# Priest for Those Who Don't Go to Church

JOHANNES AMRITZER

Original version published in Swedish by Paulus Media AB, Stockholm, Sweden, with the title Präst för de som inte går i kyrkan.


Translation: Peter Almqvist and Nina Anderson
Cover: Rickard Widell
Cover photo: Samuel Willkander and Istockphoto.com
Design: Samuel Willkander

Distributed by Paulus Media AB in cooperation with Mission SOS
Printed by Raff Printing Inc. (USA) 2010
ISBN: 978-91-977193-4-6

# Contents

## Dedication

I want to dedicate this book to all of our creative aesthetes and evangelists in the Mission SOS festival team. You preach the best message in the world. Through your unique creative gifts and talents, the Gospel of Jesus is painted to all of the still unreached people around the world at our festivals.

As Julia Willkander and Linnea Hagenfors, together with their festival band, sing down heaven on earth, jam, and create miracle faith with their pop, rock, and gospel music, I become so proud of my Jesus. All the songs are born on your knees, and your voices and purity before God stab people's hearts like daggers.

The crowds are gripped by the festive atmosphere and Jesus-feast as Anna Kvist dances and leads the dance team. The dancing allows the crowd to partake in the festival in a way that only dancing can. Through Anna and her team's movements, the isolation between Christians and non-Christians is broken, tensions are released and the audience experiences a "we" feeling. Anna has taught me to love and cherish dance. I honestly believe that there is not a more relevant instrument among people than dance. It will create a feast and make Muslims, Hindus, Buddhists, and Christians relax and laugh together. Dance can also exalt God in a unique way, and be a means for us to use our entire body. Thank you, God for blessing us with dance!

Maria Evermin helps me illustrate my sermons. Maria, along with her actors and theater monkeys, amplify the message so that no one in the audience has the courage to move. Instead they pack the area in front of the platform, stretching bodies and necks so as not to miss the mimics and drama in the performance. Bible Theater filled with creative shenanigans and fun props is something that I have become accustomed to in our festivals through the years.

I also want to dedicate this book to our media team with Samuel Willkander as the point man. Thank you for all your creativity in creating moving pictures. To all our street preachers: you love the asphalt, the concrete and more so all the people that Jesus so costly purchased through His blood. I admire you! Thank you all for making my life richer and having the guts to share the Good News of the risen Jesus with all that God has given you! Never be ashamed of being creative and happy artists – there are no better street evangelists! There is no limit to what we can do as a festival team. I love you heaps!

Your intercessor,

*Johannes Amritzer*
*President, Evangelical Mission SOS International*

## Foreword

I have heard Johannes Amritzer introduce himself as "A Priest for Those That Don't Go to Church" many times. It is, at the same time folksy and challenging – just as Johannes himself. Some of his co-workers introduce themselves in like manner. Johannes Amritzer is contagious!

When my good friend Johannes Amritzer writes about evangelization and missions he speaks straight from his heart. He is running over with zeal to present Jesus and let people that do not yet know Jesus have the chance. The world's best message must be presented in the best way possible. The word must get out! Faster! Better! More creatively and relevantly! More radically! In more places!

This book is not only a burning appeal to live in the Great Commission; it is also a manual of how Mission SOS is bringing closure to the Great Commission in a practical way. This book has many dimensions. Personally I am fascinated that this book, in all its simplicity, manages to accurately portray Johannes Amritzer and his ministry. There are stories here about Johannes' broken childhood, everyday life with Jesus, the miracles, the praises of his own team and the team's participation. The desire to reach farther and to have greater results is clearly evident. His unique calling drives him to continually hold festivals among unreached people, to train disciples and leaders, run a Mission Bible College, establish mission bases, send out missionaries, plant churches, create networks for apostolic Christianity, and now also to write books. This is the third book he has authored within twelve months. All this should be impossible to manage. The only way to explain it is an unusually large dose of the grace of God over his life!

We love you Johannes! Continue to increase the tempo. More and more are following both you and Jesus.

*Per-Olof Eurell*
*Business Man*

## Foreword by the Author

Ever since I was saved, more than 20 years ago, I have wanted to write a book on evangelism and missions. I have held back because I needed some experience first, but now the book is finally here!

The Great Commission is, of course, the most central part to us who call ourselves Christians. A Jesus-following discipleship that does not have us stretching ourselves out to those who have yet to hear, understand, or receive, lacks credibility. A self-focused or me-and-my-needs-in-focus life is honestly not worthy to be called a Christian life. Everything becomes sound, fresh, and healthy when we win people for the kingdom of God and when new disciples are trained continuously. The addition of new people, new blood, and new strength to the church is what keeps the Christian church vital, contemporary, and strong. The complete Christian life comes into the right perspective and its priorities are set right when the focus lies where Jesus intended it to be.

When we live a people-acknowledging and attractive life in the midst of society, without being ashamed of truly having the solution, every day turns into an adventure with the Holy Spirit. People long for the truth and want to get to know and listen to Christians who are genuine, who live as they teach, and who believe what is written. Introverted, navel-gazing Christianity is boring, dead, and stinks! Discussion-oriented and argumentative Christianity must be exchanged for a happy, creative, brave and winning Christianity. A new generation is growing up and a Christian cultural revolution is taking place among the European Christians. This book is one of the battle scripts of this revolution. We all need the Holy Spirit's Christian Cultural Revolution so desperately!

At the end of this book I let some of my heroes and faithful co-workers share in a couple of chapters. Wow, how much they have to say! I make no claims to be complete in my teaching on evangelism in any way. This is, on the other hand, a book written more spontaneously and straight from my heart. The book may not be that well-structured, but it shows my own and the lifestyle of Mission SOS, without filters. I hope it will be exciting reading for you! I pray that your life will be radically changed as you read.

For the unreached people and a transformed Europe and the world,

*Johannes Amritzer*
*President, Evangelical Mission SOS International*

# PART 1

CHAPTER 1

# TAKE A GREATER RESPONSIBILITY

If the Gospel of Jesus truly is the best message in the world, if this statement is true, then the church in Europe and America today is too small. In fact, the Church is way too small. Something is very strange. A system error or a locked up thought process must have blocked our God-given, fantastic brains. What is happening? Why has the Christian message not had a greater breakthrough in the last four or five generations?

The message of Jesus, His death on the cross, the resurrection, and triumph over the devil, sin, sickness, and evil is the world's best story; that is a fact! Don't be discouraged. You have not been fooled concerning the Gospel and your salvation. On the contrary, you might have been duped on the matter of the role of the church and your position of influence. You might have been duped concerning your role in this time and in your society. Yes, imagine if, in fact, you have been duped!

As a new believer I was both totally duped and dribbled away by cowardly church leaders. These leaders had basically misunderstood everything about the position of a Christian and the role of the church; they were truly lost. Poor people... A frightened, terrified, and introverted church is really double duped as the people ride a bus toward heaven in the church pews Sunday after Sunday, singing songs from the 19th century. They barely understand the meaning of the lyrics, so how much less will a non-believing guest understand? He might be wondering if he has mistaken the church for the historical cultural museum.

What do I mean by "being double duped"? Well, you see, a dull, gray, religious life is more boring than a non-Christian life. Dead religion is truly a blank in life. A fresh, healthy Jesus-centered life on the other hand, filled with the Holy Spirit and faith, is the jackpot and totally great!

## Jesus

Jesus never intended for us to isolate ourselves from our society. God so loved the world and therefore sent Jesus. He did not come to judge but to save (John 3:16-17). God loved sinners as much as saints and proved His love for sinners by letting Jesus die for them before they repented and received His salvation (Rom 5:8).

Jesus wants us to live in the world, but He does not want us to live of the world. We do not belong to the world. We, just like Jesus, were sent by God to the world to love, influence, and win! We are not afraid. We love the world but hate the spirit of the world, and have conquered it through Jesus. The Spirit of God dwells in us (1 John 4:4). Jesus prayed for us here on the earth and said in His prayer:

> *My prayer is not that you take them out of the world but that you protect them from the evil one. They are not of the world, even as I am not of it. Sanctify them by the truth; your word is truth. As you sent me into the world, I have sent them into the world.*
>
> **John 17:15-18**

Jesus had fellowship with all sorts of people and because of this He was criticized by His opponents, the self-chosen religious elite. But Jesus defended Himself accurately and said:

> *It is not the healthy who need a doctor, but the sick. I have not come to call righteous, but sinners.*
>
> **Mark 2:17**

## Abraham

The main people in the Old Testament had a strong faith in God but at the same time fellowshipped with people who practiced idol worship and completely foreign religions. These people, the believers of that time, were respected and won trust among their peers. At times they even became their spiritual guides and shepherds of their souls without compromising their radical beliefs. One example of such a man of God is the patriarch Abraham, forefather of Israel and dad of the Jews.

> *By faith Abraham, when called to go to a place he would later receive as his inheritance, obeyed and went, even though he did not know where he was going. By faith he made his home in the promised land like a stranger in a foreign country; he lived in tents, as did Isaac and Jacob, who were heirs with him of the same promise.*
>
> **Hebrews 11:8-9**

Abraham left on a wild adventure with his big family, many servants, and all his possessions to go to a land that God had promised. When Abraham arrived in this new land, there were other people living there with a completely different belief in God. Abraham did not own any property, but lived and roamed as if he already did. Abraham had a promise from God that the land would in time be his; this caused him to move and act with the kind of self-confidence that genuine faith in God's promises creates.

Early on, Abraham was also well-renowned and rewarded by the people in the land for his faith in God and his bold confession. When Abraham returned from a battle, where he also was able to rescue his nephew Lot from being kidnapped, Melchizedek, king of Salem, met with him. Melchizedek was a priest of the Most High God and we read that he said:

> *Blessed be Abram by God Most High, Creator of heaven and earth. And blessed be God Most High, who delivered your enemies into your hand.*
>
> **Gen 14:19-20**

Melchizedek recognized and confirmed that God Most High had both blessed Abraham and given him victory in battle. Melchizedek clearly saw that Abraham walked with God.

Abraham lived among the Hittites, one of the peoples in the land, with an obvious, practical, and down to earth faith that impacted and impressed all who came in contact with it. Abraham was not ashamed of his faith. Why should he have been? When his beloved wife Sarai had just died, he wanted to purchase the cave in Machpelah, at the end of a field belonging to a certain Ephron, son of Zohar.

When they were about to settle the amount to be paid, Abraham again stated that he wanted to buy the field, cave, and burial site to be able to prepare everything for his wife's funeral. Then the Hittites said that they did not want any money since Abraham had such a good reputation among them. So they allowed him to pick and choose and then take the best burial place he could find.

> *Sir, listen to us.* ***You are a mighty prince among us.*** *Bury your dead in the choicest of our tombs. None of us will refuse you his tomb for burying your dead.*
>
> **Genesis 23:6** (author's emphasis)

What are the Hittites actually saying to Abraham? What does it mean when they call Abraham a prince among us? I believe it means that they all gave Abraham their recognition as their spiritual leader; they recognized that his God was God over their gods. I also believe that they actually confessed their faith in Abraham's God. A faith in Abraham's God had at the least begun to grow within them. What an influence Abraham had! He was an alien who didn't even own property. But through his life and strong faith Abraham succeeded in winning the local inhabitants' trust. He was their spiritual leader, their guide; that's right – a prince of God among them.

Eventually Abraham was indeed able to buy the cave in Machpelah from Ephron, son of Zohar, for the price of 400 shekels of silver. Abraham now owned his first piece of property in the land that one day would belong to his descendants, fully and completely, and most certainly this land had prophetic meaning for him.

> *All these people were still living by faith when they died. They did not receive the things promised; they only saw them and welcomed them from a distance. And they admitted that they were aliens and strangers on earth.*
>
> **Hebrews 11:13**

## Daniel

The prophet Daniel is another non-compromising man of God in the Old Testament who ruled his time and locality instead of merely sitting around in a corner frightened. Daniel arrived to the superpower Babylon as a young Jew enslaved to his captives. He had to be educated, reprogrammed and brainwashed by the Chaldeans in order to work for the government. Daniel started off by deciding not to compromise his Jewish kosher rules and strangely enough won this battle with both the guard and chief official in Babylon. Daniel and his Jewish friends Hananiah, Mishael and Azariah resolved to not compromise their faith in God while they were employees of the superpower.

At one time, Daniel's three friends were thrown into a burning furnace, and Daniel himself was thrown into a lion's pit for refusing to be part of idol worship and the people's cults. God miraculously protected them and confessed to their integrity. In spite of his radical belief in the God of Israel and his bold confession thereof, Daniel was made chief over all the wise men in Babylon. These included astrologers, sorcerers and others with very dubious titles, jobs and positions. Yes, it is quite hard to digest the kind of influence that Daniel, the man of state, the counselor and the prophet, really had, both in Babylonia and later in the Persian Empire.

Nebuchadnezzar, king of Babylon, openly confessed his faith in the God of Daniel and Israel after Daniel interpreted a difficult dream for him. Nebuchadnezzar said:

> *Surely your God is the God of gods and the Lord of kings and a revealer of mysteries, for you were able to reveal this mystery. Then the king placed Daniel in a high position and lavished many gifts on him. He made him ruler over the entire province of Babylon and placed him in charge of all its wise men.*
>
> **Daniel 2:47-48**

Another time, he was thrown into a lion's pit because of his disciplined prayer life and refusal to worship the person King Darius. Daniel survived the lion's pit through angelic protection. After Daniel's night among the wild beasts, King Darius arrived at the pit anxiously shouting:

> *Daniel, servant of the living God, has your God, whom you serve continually, been able to rescue you from the lions?*
>
> **Daniel 6:20**

Darius had a great respect for Daniel's faith in God but also in Daniel's God. When he found Daniel alive among the lions, he repented and started to believe. Afterwards, my dear reader, things began to happen; this is what it says:

> *Then King Darius wrote to all the peoples, nations and men of every language throughout the land: "May you prosper greatly! I issue a decree that in every part of my kingdom people must fear and reverence the God of Daniel. For he is the living God and he endures forever; his kingdom will not be destroyed, his dominion will never end. He rescues and he saves; he performs signs and wonders in the heavens and the earth. He has rescued Daniel from the power of the lions."*
>
> **Daniel 6:25-27**

What a conversion! What faith! What a bold confession of Daniel's and Israel's God! King Darius repented to the God of Israel! God honored and confirmed Daniel's bold, uncompromising faith and his integrity was truly rewarded.

Abraham, Daniel, Joseph in Egypt and many more could be mentioned as priests among the unbelievers in the Old Testament's fascinating stories.

## Priest for Those That Do Not Go to Church

Sometime towards the end of the nineties, I sat at a restaurant in Sky City at Arlanda International Airport, just north of Stockholm, Sweden, together with some businessmen. I was on my way home from one of many trips as a missionary and was to only have a short layover at Arlanda. Then I was to continue to Sturup Airport outside of Malmö that same evening, but due to fog and wind my flight was cancelled and SAS put all of us up at SAS Radisson Hotel at Sky City.

All in all we were seven gentlemen heading toward Malmö but now stranded at Arlanda that evening. After checking into our rooms we all met again in the lobby and as a group went to spend the food vouchers that the airline had generously provided. We ended up around a table at a restaurant on the balcony at Sky City. Six businessmen and one missionary had gone out to eat together just to kill some time, all longing for home and family. None of us knew each other. Everyone was a new acquaintance.

When we had taken our seats, they all ordered beers while I had a coke. A man in his sixties, who was CEO for a large company if I recall correctly, naturally became the leader. As we awaited the food this man said: "Well, gentlemen, let's go around the table and introduce ourselves, and then we will most likely survive this evening." There were strained and polite "ha-ha's" and kind nods coming from everyone.

The leader began by stating his name, where he lived, a few words about his family, his title and then briefly shared about the company that he represented. We continued to go around the table and slowly but surely the Swedes warmed up, sipped their beers and said, "Cheers, by the way."

Then the turn came to me, last of them all. I'd had time to think it through and I said: "Well, I am a priest for those that don't go to church, with a specialty in Biblical healing and exorcism."

Dead silence around the table. Everybody stared, the leader cursed, laughed, and then said: "You're kidding, that was a good one!"

I said: "No," but also begin to laugh and then continue to explain what I mean. "There are simply too many priests for those that go to church, so we thought it was due time to ordain some full-time priests for those who don't go to church. There are many that do not go to church nowadays. Do you go to church?"

"No," they all answered simultaneously.

"Yes," I continued, "there you go! Then I am your priest!"

They laughed and were at first hesitant, but of course, I had to continue to explain what Biblical healing was and that meant a lot of Jesus for a while. Then it was all about exorcism and they became very curious. I shared miracle stories from all my missionary trips as we ate and as the men drank their beer. As the evening proceeded, their hesitation was more and more exchanged for trust toward the priest. Finally I was everyone's priest and one of the gang. I had taken my rightful position in society and had true influence.

As we walked back to the hotel one of them patted me on my back and, as we entered the lobby, said, "You are my kind of priest." I was accepted and respected. I had not had three bottles of beer, sucked up, or compromised with either my radical Jesus faith or Bible faith to win them. I had been a priest for real. I had taken a stand for Jesus, been salt in the decay, and a light in the darkness.

This later evolved into a lifestyle and a constant adventure in cooperation with the Holy Spirit. Where I live I am the community priest, where I go to shop I am known as the missionary, the priest or sometimes even the pastor. But since most people in Western Europe have no clue what a pastor is, I am most often a priest for those who do not go to church, or just simply a missionary. I love it, people love it, and the more secure I have become in this role the more obvious and fun it becomes. I own Stockholm sort of like Abraham owned Israel before it came to be the land of the Jews. Every Swede is my disciple-to-be and church member. The Swedes do not yet know that they all are part of my church, but I know, and that is enough to release a lot of immediate faith in fellowship with these wonderful people.

When I introduce myself to them as their priest that they have not yet met, we usually enjoy a good laugh together and then I ask straight away if there is something that they need help with. "What do you mean, 'help'?" they ask. I answer them by saying that if they are going through a hard time I want to be there for them, and maybe we can agree to pray for something specific. I wish you could hear the responses I get! Many times I am able to lead them in a prayer of salvation or a prayer for healing. Try it yourself! It is wonderful to take a greater responsibility. We should rule and not let ourselves be ruled. We should take over wherever we go!

Whenever I reach the scene of a disaster or accident I always make myself known as a priest or missionary. At hotels I sometimes say at the reception, "If you have an emergency you now know where to find a priest." If you can, imagine how many people are touched, even to tears sometimes, to know that a peer actual cares and puts himself in a place of disposal for his community and peers.

You, my dear reader, can also be a priest for those that do not go to church. Maybe you say, "Well, I don't work as an evangelist or pastor like you, Johannes," or, "This does not work for me." Yes it does! It is your attitude and stance toward your surroundings, the time you live in and your peers that decides if you are to be ordained or not. It is not about what job you may have. Your title is more or less useless in this circumstance; it is instead about the love of your heart toward the peers around you. We read in the book of Revelation:

> *...Jesus Christ, who is the faithful witness, and the firstborn from the dead, and the ruler of the kings of the earth. To him who loves us and has freed us from our sins by his blood, and has made us to be a kingdom and priests to serve his God and Father – to him be glory and power forever and ever! Amen.*
>
> **Revelation 1:5-6**

You are both king and priest according to the Apostle John. Start to rule your community as a small king with love and warmth. You belong to God's great kingdom! Become a priest, be a priest for all that don't go to church! Take a greater responsibility! Europe and the world need these types of Christians.

There will always be those who want to misunderstand and take this teaching over the edge. There are some who will be stubborn. So, to make sure that you will not use this book as a tool to degrade the church and its value, I will state it as clearly as possible: I believe in the church! New believers need a church. Mature Christians need the church fellowship. The local church is fantastic and God's power-broker on earth! But at the moment we are just too few in the church and we need to tear down some walls to make room for more people. This book should probably be seen as a battering-ram or a hulky sledgehammer in this new construction or clearance site.

## CHAPTER 2

# WHAT A LITTLE LOVE CAN DO

I moved in with a support family at the age of six, together with both my brother Karl and my dad Ewald, who at the time was an emotional wreck. The Franklin family opened up their home in Taberg, Sweden for several very intense months during an extremely turbulent season in the Amritzer family. My parents had separated after months of turbulence and intrigues. My dad Ewald and I, along with my siblings from his first marriage, Karl and Anna, had spent some time in Austria at our Grandmother Anna's place as well as at Aunt Elvira's place.

Upon our return from Austria we had nowhere to live, so my dad, Karl and I moved in with the Franklins. Young Anna moved in with Mom. My parents were now in the middle of a divorce and trying to sort everything out, from partition of joint property to who would be the legal guardian of the kids, all with help from a lawyer and the local social welfare office. It was a dark season with a lot of fights, scenes and tears from us all. The Franklins were guardian angels. They had a full house: their own children Mona and Patrik, their prior foster children Kent, Stefan, and Tord; yet they still received us into their home. They already had extra people staying at their house: Lasse and Lolita; Jimmy, Mona's boyfriend; plus four large sheep dogs. And we must not forget Lasse's collie... what a wonderful mess! What great and warmhearted people! Yes, it was truly a large family in the '70s style. The Franklins attended the Mission Church in Taberg and most likely lived this out-giving, self-sacrificing life due to their Christian faith.

I was supposed to sleep in a sofa bed in the billiard room, but the first night it was very hard to fall asleep, I longed so much for Mom, Grandma and Aunt Elvira that I cried in bed. I had already moved so much and had been thrown among families and people that all wanted to help. I recall how all the shadows in the room turned to ghosts, and I did not have the courage to call for Eina – that was Mrs. Franklin – to come. I didn't know her yet, even though time would show what a wonderful person she was. She had a great heart, especially for kids.

All of a sudden, an angel stepped through the door to the billiard room. It was not an angel with two golden candles in his hands, but a thirteen-year-old, long haired boy with a glass of milk in one hand and a battery in the other. He licked the battery every now and then to get a rush. It was Stefan. Stefan was one of the Franklin's foster kids and my new idol! Immediately I sat up in bed and wiped the tears from my eyes.

Stefan turned on a light, handed me the glass of milk and abruptly said: "Drink this and you'll see that you'll go to sleep."

It sounded as if it was a magical potion, but the milk was not even spiked, I promise! He sat down next to the bed and smiled. The smile almost made the patch of tobacco under his upper lip fall out, but he quickly caught it with his tongue and pushed it back into place.

"Stefan," I thought. "How good of him to come. I like him!"

Earlier that day he had given me a tour of the big yellow house. And in the large pantry, Stefan had showed my where the sugar cubes, the dog candy, and the dog food were kept. To impress me, he had downed a full bag of dog food. It was not a big one, only 750 grams, but still, that's an achievement. Back then the ingredients of dog food were likely ground carcasses, fish flour and other yummy stuff. I had laughed so hard that I had gotten a tummy ache and I almost wet my pants; as a six-year-old, "almost" means only a little bit.

Later that day when Stefan was sitting next to my bed, I handed him the empty glass and looked at him with eyes red from crying.

He then said the magic words: "I will sit here until you fall asleep."

Wow! That felt so good as I crawled under the blanket again. Stefan started to tell bedtime stories about beheaded men and flowers on tombstones that some invisible phenomena had placed there, even though they had been guarded all night and no one had seen anything.

Real kid-friendly wouldn't you say?! Stefan came every night during our stay at the Franklin's. Till this day I do not know why, but he came with a glass of milk or yogurt in one hand, battery in the other and an oversized patch of tobacco under his upper lip. He sat there every night telling me ghost stories until I fell asleep. Perhaps he saw himself in me.

What do you think happens in a young boy as this plays out? I began to love Stefan, yes, to almost adore him. I wanted to be just like him, to walk like him. I wanted to look like him, do tobacco like him, be him. I would ride with him on a moped they had in the forest. I always hung on tightly to him or ran up as close as I could. I tried to do tobacco but threw up behind the garage. I could not give back much as a six-year-old kid, but I was loved anyway, loved because I was a child.

Stefan and I never met again during our childhood and our lives went in very different directions. Several years passed before I met him again. This time, it was on a beach alongside a small Swedish lake. I was twenty-two and he must have been at least twenty-nine. He had a beer in hand and sat on his towel next to his girlfriend and his German Shepherd. I walked up and said a happy hello but he did not recognize me. I introduced myself as the young Austrian boy, Ewald's boy, who had stayed with the Franklins for a short period at the end of the seventies. I tried to get him to remember me.

Yes, then he recalled. We looked at each other but did not have anything to say to each other; we did not have much in common except for some warm memories from an otherwise tragic childhood. Actually we both probably wanted to give the other a hug, but two men in shorts on a beach did not hug back then in Sweden. Instead we sat there together on our towels and felt a deep fellowship and love for one another without the need for many words.

As I got in my car to ride home that afternoon, the Holy Spirit spoke to me: "What you just experienced is the power of unconditional love, Johannes."

That love impacts and leaves deep tracks in a person. After all these years I feel a river of gratitude and love flow through me when I think of Stefan sitting on the edge of the sofa bed in the billiard room in Taberg. I see him sitting there in the Franklin home with an empty glass of milk in his hand. Tears begin to flow as I think of him: long hair, t-shirt with a heavy metal emblem, jean jacket, an oversized patch of tobacco under his upper lip, licking that gross battery. That is true love! Stefan is a warm memory from my otherwise dark childhood.

Imagine what a little love can do. Think of the deep tracks that love can leave in a person. Thank you, Stefan! There is such a power in unconditional love. That kind of love is pure and strong. It comes from God. God loves the world. God loves unconditionally. God loves sinners and those who do wrong. God's love is enormous.

> *For God so loved the world that he gave his one and only Son, that whoever believes in him shall not perish but have eternal life.*
>
> **John 3:16**

> *... God is love.*
>
> **1 John 4:8b**

*Dear friends, let us love one another, for love comes from God. Everyone who loves has been born of God and knows God. Whoever does not love does not know God*

**1 John 4:7-8a**

There is a natural chain reaction in love and a great power that changes us as humans. The chain reaction looks something like this:

1. God attacks us and loves us completely and uncon ditionally, without control or limit!

*But God demonstrates his own love for us in this: While we were still sinners, Christ died for us.*

**Romans 5:8**

*This is love: not that we loved God, but that he loved us and sent his Son as an atoning sacrifice for our sins.*

**1 John 4:10**

2. We cannot help loving God back; there is nothing else to do but love Him. We return His love by loving.

*But he who has been forgiven little loves little.*

**Luke 7:47b**

I, for my part, have been forgiven so much and therefore love God very much. Oh, how I love Him!

*"The most important one," answered Jesus, "is this: 'Hear, O Israel, the Lord our God, the Lord is one. Love the Lord your God with all your heart and with all your soul and with al your mind and with all your strength.'"*

**Mark 12:29-30**

**3.** We begin to love people around us just as God has loved and loves us.

*We love because He first loved us.*

**1 John 4:19**

*Dear friends, since God so loved us, we also ought to love one another.*

**1 John 4:11**

*The second is this: 'Love your neighbor as yourself.'*

**Mark 12:31**

Yes, that is the way it is! The apostle Paul lived his life for Him who loved him much:

*I have been crucified with Christ and I no longer live, but Christ lives in me. The life I live in the body, I live by faith in the Son of God, who loved me and gave himself for me.*

**Galatians 2:20**

The apostle Paul was completely driven by love for God and people in his ministry as apostle, missionary and church builder. He was in love with God but also with people. He who does not love people will never be able to convey the message of love from God to the people. Paul was crazy about God and therefore driven by His kind of empathy and love. Paul says:

> *If we are out of our mind, it is for the sake of God; if we are in our right mind, it is for you. For Christ's love compels us...*
>
> **2 Corinthians 5:13-14b**

Preaching the Gospel of Jesus without love cannot be done, it is impossible! The Gospel is God's declaration of love to humanity. The Bible is God's love letter to you and me. He wrote the last part, the New Testament, with His own blood as the ink and one of the nails from the cross as the pen. The Gospel of Jesus is saturated with, vibrates, and sends out pulses of love, only love.

When we begin to love the way Jesus loves, we release the greatest transforming power in the universe. The real great power dwells within the great love. There are actually no impossible, hopeless cases among people, nor are there hard, tough geographical places, only a lack of love. Love breaks through, makes ground, finds a way, and makes room! The apostle Paul says of love:

> *It always protects, always trusts, always hopes, always perseveres.*
>
> **1 Corinthians 13:7**

## Love Miracles

During the summer of 1993 I worked in the city of Gorlitz, in the eastern parts of Germany close to the Polish border. Even though this was two or three years after the reconciliation of East and West Germany, not much had happened in these eastern-most parts of former East Germany except for a greater availability of food and the addition of new gas stations everywhere. Everything still had the old East Germany feel. The streets were worn down cobblestone and the apartment buildings were beyond repair where the coatings were almost gone. Everything was black or gray due to the use of coal. On the streets there were only old cars of the makes Trabant, Skoda and Lada. Each family raised rabbits and hens in their backyard, even in the middle of the city, just to make ends meet. German Neo Nazi gangs fought Polish gangs over the rule of the streets and city blocks. Alcohol, drugs, and prostitutes were sold everywhere and very openly. Today Gorlitz is an idyllic and a fantasy town, back then it was a sweaty armpit of old East Germany.

I worked in the European team of Teen Challenge. I had been a street evangelist for the past twelve months and had already worked in several places in Eastern Europe, mainly in Poland. I felt at home in East Germany and I was able to speak German, which I loved. I had been a Christian for three years and preached for just over one. Life was great! We held street meetings, tent meetings outside the city, and went from apartment to apartment sharing the Gospel with Polish whores, German Neo Nazis and poor Gypsies.

We quickly made friends with a German gang that we played soccer with after they agreed to come to our meetings. We played them and won, and the gang lived up to their word and came to the meetings. The only problem was that they were drunk and did their best to destroy as much as possible. They kicked down our outhouse behind the tent and jumped on the roof of the American guest speaker's rental car. They also beat up a young girl so that we had to take her to the ER in the middle of our service because of a broken jaw.

One of the skinheads, Mario, twenty-four years old, stole the attention at one of our street meetings by dancing in the fountain. Mario continued to steal the attention while I was preaching at night by dancing up the middle aisle in the tent with an orange traffic cone on his head, yelling: "Save me, Priest, save me!"

I am not exaggerating, once I had to duck a flying beer bottle while I was preaching. By now you probably understand that it was not easy to love these "meeting terrorists." I remember us praying and fasting for five days, asking God for a breakthrough in the city. I think we rebuked every demon power between Hamburg and Munich. I lost my temper in the middle of the fasting and almost punched a guy who was more than cocky. Wow, how ashamed I felt afterwards as I let go of his t-shirt and said a hypocritical, "Jesus loves you." The truth was, I felt no love for him at all, but Jesus did.

Mario's gang disturbed us again by hosting a party in the apartment below the one our team leased. At least that is what it felt like. We went to bed around midnight but there was no way to go to sleep due to all the noise from the apartment below.

The old East German building had thin walls and bad floors. The subwoofers in the stereo system pounded and blended with drunken loudness.

At three AM there was a knock on the door. Two of us opened the outside door to the dark stairway, where two gang members that we by this time knew very well, stood. They asked us to come down to take care of Mario who had supposedly passed out. Against better judgment we followed them down and I said something like, "I am definitely not a psychologist with Birkenstock sandals and round spectacles, but a faith preacher with a black belt in spiritual warfare." I continued to whine, saying that they could come and visit when they were sober but not at three AM when they were wasted. But on the inside I knew that this could be our chance for a breakthrough and acted more on instinct and intuition than on will and sound judgment.

We grabbed Mario in the midst of vomit, bottles, overflowing ashtrays, dancing, making out, drunken German teens and young adults. We dragged him up all the stairs. Mario stunk; he had probably not changed clothes in a couple of weeks, and we decided to give him a bath that he would never forget. It all began like a practical joke as we locked ourselves into the bathroom. The guys in the team laughed as we took off all his clothes and threw them in the washing machine and dumped him naked and unconscious in the tub. We joked about washing him with harsh soap and steel wool because he sure did stink. We started off with cold water but when he did not wake up we began using lukewarm water and almost an entire bottle of shampoo.

We were scrubbing and shaving him when it happened; we were on our knees leaning over the tub when we felt the presence of the Holy Spirit so strongly in the bathroom. The Spirit of Jesus filled us and Mario became a man in ruins that Jesus loves. All of a sudden we saw ourselves in Mario and realized that this was exactly how God loved us and what He did for us in salvation. Mario did not deserve the treatment that we were giving him and neither did we deserve salvation. We continued to wash and scrub and as we did tears began to roll down my cheeks and fall into the water.

The love miracle happened; it took place right in front of us. To this day, we do not understand fully what happened that night. We dried Mario with a towel; put some deodorant and Barracuda aftershave on him. We dressed him in my clothes and seated him in a chair in the next room. As he slowly regained consciousness, we tried to feed him some coffee and sandwiches but to no avail.

> *A new command I give you: Love one another. As I have loved you, so you must love one another. By this all men will know that you are my disciples, if you love one another.*
>
> **John 13:34-35**

Early that morning the entire team sat in a circle around Mario, all smiling. The wonderful presence of the Holy Spirit filled the room. We wanted to cry, laugh, pray, worship and rejoice at once because the Spirit was present and filling us to the rim. We had found gold in the cliff. We had found oil in the sea. We had won the lottery jackpot. We understood that we now were part of something wonderful but still had no idea what it was.

Sometimes we just know that we have done something that God really likes, and we can sense it in our whole body. All of a sudden we are surprised by the favor and presence of God. I had searched for the great power in Christianity for three years and had just found it, all of a sudden, in the great love. If any blind or deaf people had been present in the room, they would instantly have been healed; if there had been demon possessed there, the demons would not have been able to hide anymore. How do I know this? Well, because the presence in that room was the same compact presence of the Holy Spirit that we have felt in our festivals as the wave of miracles and deliverances passes through the hungry crowd. I know what I am talking about. That night I had abruptly found the miracle power in the great love for Jesus and for people.

When Mario slowly began to understand and grasp what had happened, as he began to sober up and see that we had washed him, dressed him in my clothes, and shaved him, it was just too overwhelming for him. He started to cry and say, while running out of the apartment: "What have you done? Have you touched me?"

Two days later Mario returned and knocked on our door. He had had two beers just in order to gain the courage to speak to me, and he tried desperately to act tough as he confronted me. He said that we had disgraced him and disrespected his integrity. I tilted my head and simply said that we only tried to show the same love that Jesus once showed us. Then and there the message of Jesus penetrated his heart; the Word became flesh for him; he understood.

Mario pushed me to the side and ran in to the kitchen, grabbed a chair and fell on his knees crying out, "Help me, Johannes!" I knelt down next to him and led him in a prayer of salvation.

A couple of days later we baptized Mario in a small pool of water in Gorlitz, and several others joined him; more and more were giving their lives to Jesus as a result of Mario's salvation. In less than two weeks, about seventy people received salvation and forty of them received the baptism of the Holy Spirit and immediately began to speak in tongues. (It tickles as you place your hand on the head of a skinhead who wants to be baptized in the Holy Spirit and fire!) A new church was established as a result of that summer evangelism.

I turned twenty that summer and my evangelistic ministry exploded as a result of the breakthrough in Eastern Germany. A wave of love miracles followed me everywhere I preached. I had gotten my hands on the love dynamics of the Spirit of Jesus and breakthrough after breakthrough followed in nation after nation. Powerful demon deliverances and healing miracles have since then always taken place when I have preached the Gospel of Jesus, saturated with love.

At the end of the '90s I did some traveling in Russia. In 1998 I preached in an old cultural palace about 250 miles north of Moscow. It was one of those wild and wonderful nights where I began joking with the Russians and could not stop. Warm, simple and raw jokes warmed up the audience and when the altar call for salvation went out everyone wanted intercession.

I prayed for and prophesied over everyone in the building, around 500 in number.

After two hours I realized that I was about to pray for a certain babushka for the third time. I recognized her by the red scarf she was wearing. I then said to her despondently, "I have already prayed and prophesied over you twice, isn't that enough?"

"No," she answered. Then she cried out in a loud voice with tears rolling down her cheeks, "None of us want to go home, because you are a priest that truly loves us!"

The entire building agreed with her through rejoicing and applause. I received a knife in my heart through the warm, honor-reception from the elderly Russian lady. I laughed, cried, and continued to pray for people, I do not know for how long. A deaf ear was opened and evil spirits left people! Imagine what a little love can do.

## CHAPTER 3

# A Winning Lifestyle

Apostle Paul challenges the Christians of Colosse to live in a special way. We understand that Paul shares from his well-proven experience which had become his own lifestyle through the years. After authoring almost half of the New Testament, Paul must be worthy of being taken seriously and listened to, am I right? The apostle, missionary, and church planter says:

> *Devote yourselves to prayer, being watchful and thankful. And pray for us, too, that God may open a door for our message, so that we may proclaim the mystery of Christ, for which I am in chains. Pray that I may proclaim it clearly, as I should. Be wise in the way you act toward outsiders; make the most of every opportunity. Let your conversation be always full of grace, seasoned with salt, so that you may know how to answer everyone.*
>
> **Colossians 4:2-6**

What is Apostle Paul actually saying? Well yes, these are great tips on how we should live winning and evangelizing lives. By a winning life I mean a Spirit-filled Christian life that has an attraction force on unbelievers, and that also has the ability to make them into disciples. Let us break these verses down and study them part by part together.

## 1. Never Stop Praying

*Devote yourselves to prayer...*

**Colossians 4:2a**

Prayer makes all the difference in evangelism. When we pray for the people we share the Gospel with, the Holy Spirit works in them, our relationship and ourselves. If we only take a few minutes of every day to pray for those that we want to win, they will soften up, become more open and curious. We also become better and more open channels for the Spirit of God when we spend time with God in prayer.

During the late '90s my wife and I lived just south of Möllevången, a suburb of Malmö in southern Sweden. We lived in the same stairway as 17-year-old twins Nina and Davor and their mom. Our kitchen window faced the inner yard. Every morning, about 7:30, Nina and Davor came walking across the yard on their way to school. Davor lit a cigarette and Nina carried a heavy green duffel bag for her Karate practice. Once she reached the coded gate, Nina held it up and waited for her brother, yelling for him to hurry up. The procedure was the same every morning: Davor would light his cigarette and Nina would have to wait.

I watched them from my kitchen, where I was praying. I smiled and laughed at them; they were so innocent. As the gate closed with a slam and they hurried off to school, I would lift my hands and pray, "God, give me a chance to share the Gospel with them! Holy Spirit, do Your work! Let me lead them to salvation!" As I prayed, a deep compassion and love for the twins from Croatia was born in my heart.

It was not long before I got to know them and Davor would come over and we would watch a movie or play some video games. I agreed to instruct one of Davor's friends who was attempting to get his driver's license. His name was Erdjan and he was from Bosnia, living in Sweden without his dad. We had fun in the car and enjoyed ourselves, even if Erdjan almost killed us at times. Other times Davor and I went shooting clay pigeons. What a guy! Davor was very soft and open to the Gospel from the start. His sister on the other hand had a tougher surface. But she thawed fast and I noticed that she had the world's largest heart. After six months or so I was able to lead them both to salvation.

We focus on the task when we pray for the fulfillment of the Great Commission. Consistent and persistent prayer really makes a difference. Prayer is to turn people over to the influence of the Spirit of God. You have to believe in the work of the Holy Spirit! Salvation is actually a miracle, a sign that God performs in a person's heart.

*I am not ashamed of the gospel, because it is the power of God for the salvation of everyone who believes...*

**Romans 1:16a**

The Gospel is the power of God that saves (1 Corinthians 1:18, 2:5, 4:20).

*The god of this age has blinded the minds of unbelievers, so that they cannot see the light of the gospel of the glory of Christ...*

**2 Corinthians 4:4a**

Paul stated that the devil, enemy to both God and mankind, has made the people on the earth blind to the Gospel of Jesus. When we pray we can remove the filthy blanket of the devil and open the spiritually blind eyes, enabling people to see Jesus and what He has done for them. This is called spiritual warfare.

*For though we live in the world, we do not wage war as the world does. The weapons we fight with are not the weapons of the world. On the contrary, they have divine power to demolish strongholds. We demolish arguments and every pretension that sets itself up against the knowledge of God...*

**2 Corinthians 10:3-5a**

All different kinds of isms: Atheism, Humanism, Materialism, Post Modernism and religions and philosophies like Hinduism and Confucianism are strongholds and edifices of ideas. We need to tear down these edifices in people's minds using our spiritual weapons in prayer, but also through conversations and preaching.

> *For our struggle is not against flesh and blood, but against the rulers, against the authorities, against the powers of this dark world and against the spiritual forces of evil in the heavenly realms.*
>
> **Ephesians 6:12**

Jesus won the battle for mankind's salvation on the cross of Calvary two thousand years ago. Everything is complete! Nothing needs to be added. The salvation has been fully accomplished! People just do not see clearly. That is why we need to fight against blinding demon powers and break down edifices of ideas so that the people can hear, see clearly, and receive the salvation that comes with the Gospel. Theoretically, all people are already saved, they just need to receive repentance and believe for salvation to become a reality in their lives (1 Peter 2:24). Salvation becomes a reality when a person makes key choices to both repent and believe by faith.

Spiritual warfare and strong prayer combined with evangelism are fantastic! But spiritual warfare without evangelism soon becomes elitism. Elitist Christianity is a poor, stinking, introverted, charismatic Christianity – a strange or weird Christianity, to tell you the truth. On the other hand, evangelism without prayer and spiritual warfare becomes dry, overly intellectual and powerless. We need to practice both in a strong combination in order to have real spiritual and physical breakthrough.

## 2. A Positive Expectation

*...being watchful and thankful.*

**Colossians 4:2b**

Also, have a positive expectation in prayer and when meeting unbelievers. This is so important! When I take my children fishing I make sure I take them to waters where I know there is a good catch – otherwise they lose faith and interest very fast. It needs to be exciting the whole time. The Holy Spirit wants to take you to these kinds of waters if you pray with both a positive and thankful expectation and keep your eyes open. Watchful prayer with thanksgiving is praying in the midst of evangelization. When I pray with thanksgiving I quickly move over into the prophetic and often start to prophesy in my prayers.

It can sound like this: "Thank You, God for letting Nina receive both salvation and the baptism in the Holy Spirit tomorrow night! Thank You, God that Your Spirit is influencing her now!"

When I am out hunting deer, I continuously search the slash or the pasture watchfully and expectantly from my hideout up in a tree or tower or on my belly up on a hill. I would not go out hunting if I did not think I was going to shoot something. I do not get to shoot every time but probably every third time. Likewise, be a Christian that believes in the great catch and also believe that you will bring something home when you are out hunting souls for the Kingdom of God! The Spirit of God will point you to a person that is as ripe as an overgrown raspberry that has already fallen from the bush, if you listen to Him. On the train, bus, airplane, at the café or your job – there are people everywhere that are ripe and ready to be harvested! Your positive expectation makes a great difference.

## 3. Open Doors

*And pray for us, too, that God may open a door for our message...*

**Colossians 4:3a**

A door for the word, yes, God can truly open such doors for us if we pray. A door is opened to a specific people group or to a nation and, all of a sudden, we are given the opportunity to share the Gospel of Jesus to thousands of people who repent and come to Jesus. Apostle Paul says:

*...because a great door for effective work has opened to me…*

**1 Corinthians 16:9a**

In 2007 God opened such a door for us in Mission SOS to the Kingdom of Lesotho, a small mountainous country landlocked by South Africa. The king and queen were the invitees and a minister from the government gave a speech at the inaugural service at Maseru Soccer Stadium. During our first visit, about 9,000 people were saved and 80 demon possessed were set free.

The healing miracles were uncountable; many blind, deaf, and crippled were healed! A HIV-positive woman suffering from AIDS was declared well by a medical doctor after her blood tested HIV-negative. What happened? One of our street evangelists had laid hands on her and prayed a prayer of healing in the name of Jesus! She danced for joy with me on the platform and the crowd rejoiced! Seventeen new tent churches were started directly after the Blood of Life Festival and the door remained open to this nation as we returned for the Maseru Signs & Wonders Festival the following year! I was even invited to the palace for a Bible Study with King Letsie III and Queen M'asenate. I prophesied over them and prayed with them for the situation of their nation. Another 6,000 people were saved at this second festival and uncountable miracles took place. God had opened a door for the Gospel!

> *... See, I have placed before you an open door that no one can shut...*
>
> **Revelation 3:8**

## 4. Correct Language

> *...that I may proclaim it clearly, as I should.*
>
> **Colossians 4:4**

It is completely necessary that we speak the correct language when communicating with people. If we want to reach a Hindu man in rural Uttar Pradesh in northern India, we cannot speak

Spanish, but rather Hindi or a local tribal language. If we are delivering an important message and really want the listener to understand, we speak Swedish to a Swede and Danish to a Dane, not English. Even though we Scandinavians both understand and speak English to a degree, nothing compares to our mother tongue when trying to convey nuances. Nuances and details are important when we preach and convey the Gospel. If the latter is not important to God, why did He let the people in Jerusalem, on the day of Pentecost, the birthday of the church, hear the disciples speak about the mighty works of God in their native languages?

> *Then how is it that each of us hears them in his own native language?*
>
> **Acts 2:8**

Speaking the correct language and being culturally relevant to those that need the Gospel was so important to Apostle Paul that he asked God to help him in this art. This is the handiwork of every missionary, like a wooden sculpture that never seems to be ready. We work on, polish and improve details all the time. I constantly work on being culturally relevant and to always use the correct language with everyone that I meet. Avoiding church vocabulary as much as possible is great, but it is better yet to never learn this introverted and stupid language. Speak the language of your peers and live with and in your time. "God help me to be relevant, reaching the people without compromising!" That is my constant prayer!

## 5. Right Conduct

*Be wise in the way you act toward outsiders...*

**Colossians 4:5a**

It is obvious that we cannot constantly be moral and ethical police and know-it-all's in our fellowship with neighbors and colleagues who have yet to receive salvation. But to not take part and laugh at their sex and racist jokes, their way of speech or not to partake in their gossip is just as important. Follow the Holy Spirit and show a lot of love; that is usually the best way to act reasonably. Be someone that your unsaved friends like to hang out with and laugh together with. Humor and little mischiefs are unbeatable in fellowship with unsaved relatives, neighbors and colleagues.

## 6. Do Not Miss Your Chance

*... make the most of every opportunity.*

**Colossians 4:5b**

God gives us many chances to share the Gospel with people in close proximity to us all the time. If you have missed a train, just remain at the platform, do not go anywhere; there are more trains coming. After some time you will become more and more skilled at holding on to the chances that both God and life throws your way. Do not forget that the Holy Spirit is on your team and that He is longing to pass the ball to you in order to make you one happy goal scorer. The Holy Spirit wants to give you chances at the gas station, in the grocery store, as you meet your neighbor on your way home from the laundromat or when you are out walking your dog. The Holy Spirit wants to give you chances at the pool, the gym, in the park and during coffee break at work.

## 7. Spice Up Your Speech

> *Let your conversation be always full of grace, seasoned with salt, so that you may know how to answer everyone.*
>
> **Colossians 4:6**

Friendly but seasoned with salt, what does that mean? It means that Christians do not need to be the sissys or the mockeries that everyone laughs at in the workplace. We can be normal yet radical and bold and dare to speak out truths when need be. We need to be Christians who take part in the community debates, who dare to say that abortion is murder, and that you should get married and not just live together if you love one another. Christians who dare to say no to taking jobs under the table, dare to say no to receiving money on the side and who stand up against xenophobia and racism are needed both in Europe and in the US. More Christians with backbones are needed!

A great Christian leader was on national TV in Germany and the journalist asked what he thought about homosexuality.

The preacher answered that the Bible clearly states that homosexuality is abnormal sexuality and perversion.

The journalist continued and asked: "What do you think?"

The preacher answered: "I believe what the Bible says. When I go to fill up my car I do not put the nozzle in the exhaust pipe but in the right hole."

The journalist laughed so hard that he could barely continue the interview. On another occasion the same preacher was asked what he thought about alcohol being used for medicinal purposes. "Is not a little wine or liquor good for the stomach?" he was asked.

The preacher answered: "There was a man who had a problem with his whining and complaining wife. He went down to the local bar to take a few beers to help him forget about his marriage problems. When he returned home he had double vision and now had two whining and complaining wives." Everyone laughed.

The preacher then said, "Alcohol is a bad medicine and never helps anyone but has, on the other hand, ruined many people's lives. Alcohol is a curse." This Christian leader could really answer well, radically yet folksy, with humor and warmth.

CHAPTER 4

# Checklist for Missionaries

Mission SOS sends out missionaries to unreached people groups. Before departing on their faith adventure in life they are trained at SOS Mission Bible College in Stockholm, Sweden or MCM Ministry School in Pittsburgh, Pennsylvania. Most of the missionaries-to-be as well as the missionaries presently at home are very ambitious and serious and therefore do their own research. They study the language and prepare in different ways before they depart. Their goal, of course, is to become the best missionaries in the world.

I believe that we need to start thinking like missionaries in our home nations as well. What if, for a while, we all dwelled on the thought of actually being missionaries at home and not only in a faraway place on the mission field? If we ponder that thought I think that we would all act completely different from the way we act today. Ok, now consider that you are a missionary when you go to work, meet your neighbors, go to the gym, shop and have a hair cut! Then we need to study what a Biblical missionary does in everyday life and write down a checklist. How did Paul live, for example? If we were actually to apply the lifestyle of Paul and his way of working to our daily lives, we would truly reach a long way.

In the Book of Acts, the first history book of the church, we read about when Paul preached the gospel of Jesus in Asia and Europe during the 40's, 50's, and 60's of the first century. Paul was sent out as an apostle (Greek) or missionary (apostle in Latin) from the church in Antioch, which was a strong missions and miracle center at that time. The Antioch fellowship was a multicultural and international church that was full of life and had a mission pulse. During his second mission trip Paul arrived in the capital and center of the Hellenistic world, the legendary old Athens. He was already a fairly experienced missionary when met with yet another unreached people group. How did he proceed? We read:

> *The men who escorted Paul brought him to Athens and then left with instructions for Silas and Timothy to join him as soon as possible.*
>
> **Acts 17:15**

There had been riots in both of the Greek cities of Thessalonica and Berea due to Paul's bold preaching. In secret, Paul's team brought him to Athens, away from the violence and murder conspiracies. Paul's closest worker at the time, Silas, and Paul's spiritual son, Timothy, finished the team's work and commitments in Berea and were set to join him as soon as possible in Athens. In the meantime, Paul commenced the pioneer and mission work in Athens on his own. He had done this in the past and probably enjoyed working solo for a couple of days. He wandered through the city. Paul undertook a spiritual expedition on Christian virgin ground and did his own research. It says:

> *While Paul was waiting for them in Athens, he was greatly distressed to see that the city was full of idols.*
>
> **Acts 17:16**

## 1. Discipline Your Spirit

We read that Paul was upset when he saw all the idolatry and temples. He was upset in his spirit. Of course! He was a man of prayer and fasting, accustomed to casting out demons, performing miracles and acts of power in the name of Jesus and the power of the Holy Spirit. The Spirit of God within his spirit reacted to all the demonic activity in the city. Paul's discernment was on high alert and his "demon radar" was exposing activity all around. Paul and the demons both knew that a confrontation was at hand; a man of God had come to town.

Paul moved through town, criss-crossing between the temples like a nuclear-armed submarine. The Spirit of God within him was ready to detonate with authority and power at any time, if Paul chose to fire. But he chose not to fire. He instead did what every missionary must learn. He disciplined his own spirit. No Spirit-filled Christian needs to prophecy just because the Spirit has a message, or cast out the devil from a poor victim just because the demons roar a little.

*The spirits of prophets are subject to the control of prophets.*

**1 Corinthians 14:32**

If I wish to win and help a stripper or prostitute that might be full of demons, then I first of all need to discipline myself in order to win her trust. When she later asks for help, we cast out the devils and set her free! If I want to win a Hindu guru, I cannot begin by spitting on his Shiva or Ganesha temple. If I want to win a Muslim, I cannot curse his mosque. If I want to win a north European, I cannot frown when the Swede or Finn empties his Vodka bottle, swears and sings cheer ballads. If I wish to win, I need to learn how to discipline my highly explosive spirit and choose to detonate at the opportune place and time. There is a time to hold back and a time to go for it. Hallelujah for going for it!

## 2. Build Relations With All Kinds of People

*So he reasoned in the synagogue with the Jews and the God-fearing Greeks, as well as in the marketplace day by day with those who happened to be there. A group of Epicurean and Stoic philosophers began to dispute with him. Some of them asked, "What is this babbler trying to say?" Others remarked, "He seems to be advocating foreign gods." They said this because Paul was preaching the good news about Jesus and the resurrection.*

**Acts 17:17-18**

We read that Paul conversed with the Jews and the Gentiles that revered the God of Israel, probably in conjunction with the synagogue in the city. Paul also spent a considerable amount of time with the Greek philosophers and the Hellenistic seekers that he found on the city square. After a couple of days Paul became a well known face among the Athenians. The well-experienced missionary knew how to create curiosity and therefore build relationships with all types of people and people groups. He fellowshipped with Jews, Greeks, the learned, the uneducated, Rabbis, philosophers, store owners, and restaurant owners. A true missionary knows how to build relationships with anyone and everyone and loves all people.

Different cultures and society levels are, by the way, very fascinating and exciting connections and lessons! Life is so enriched if we have the courage to fellowship with all people. Paul was bold to share the gospel of Jesus and the resurrection right away and not after three years of dopey relationship building. He did not prevaricate or muffle the message, instead he went straight for the smash after just a few courtesy phrases and some encouraging words on the city's architecture and art. Build relations, take time to create an opening and trust, but do not hide your faith, be straightforward. If you wait too long with your confession, people will feel conned when you tell them that you are actually a missionary and Jesus follower. Honesty and openness will always serve you well.

## 3. Favor, Curiosity, and the Non-Christian's Place of Influence

*Then they took him and brought him to a meeting of the Areopagus, where they said to him, "May we know what this new teaching is that you are presenting? You are bringing some strange ideas to our ears, and we want to know what they mean." (All the Athenians and the foreigners who lived there spent their time doing nothing but talking about and listening to the latest ideas.)*

**Acts 17:19-21**

The different representatives for the large lines of philosophy and persons with great influence and high positions among the seekers in Athens invited Paul to come and hold a seminar on the Christian faith. He was invited to the Areopagus. The Areopagus was situated on a hill due northwest of Acropolis, the place where the High Court in Athens adjourned. The Areopagus acted as an ancient lineage place of lecture. It was held in high status among the intellectuals in the city; not everyone was invited. From this, we understand that the missionary Paul received their favor and managed to create such a curiosity that the Greeks gave him their own platform. Through this invitation Paul received both great recognition as well as significant influence within the city. God can give us this type of favor among Muslims, Hindus, Buddhists, New Age people, Animistic tribal people, politicians, athletes, businessmen, Punks, Goths, and children.

## 4. Greek to the Greeks

*Paul then stood up in the meeting of the Areopagus and said: "Men of Athens! I see that in every way you are very religious.*

**Acts 17:22**

The Apostle Paul truly lived as he taught and knew how effective one sentence could be. By speaking their language, coupling with their special styles and by using their own codes, he could unlock a people. The gestures, tone, choice of words and behavior, everything was thought through and sensitively adjusted to the Greek audience. In one of his letters, Paul taught the newly saved Greeks and said with such accuracy:

*Though I am free and belong to no man, I make myself a slave to everyone, to win as many as possible. To the Jews I became like a Jew, to win the Jews. To those under the law I became like one under the law (though I myself am not under the law), so as to win those under the law. To those not having the law I became like one not having the law (though I am not free from God's law but am under Christ's law), so as to win those not having the law. To the weak I became weak, to win the weak. I have become all things to all men so that by all possible means I might save some. I do all this for the sake of the gospel that I may share in its blessings.*

**1 Corinthians 9:19-23**

No price is too high to pay when it comes to reaching new people groups with the Gospel. If we need to let our hair grow, then okay, if we need to shave it off, then we'll do that. If we need to remove the piercing in the lower lip or eyebrow, or take out the ring from the ear, then okay, no problem! Some need to remove the tie at times – come on, man, take off your tie! Suit at times (sigh), jeans at times (wonderful) and bare feet in clogs (great!)

Paul's opening phrase as he began his speech to the Greek audience at the Areopagus was brilliant, excellent and so winning: "Men of Athens! I see that in every way you are very religious." Yes, as that was said, every head in the audience nodded with approval and the philosophers beamed in satisfaction. That was exactly what they wanted to hear and what they wanted to be: "very religious." He won their trust and got their attention immediately after he had greeted them. He said, "hello," and the philosophers were eating out of his hand! What an outstanding missionary!

## 5. Points of Contact, Bridges and Analogies

*For as I walked around and looked carefully at your objects of worship, I even found an altar with this inscription: TO AN UNKNOWN GOD. Now what you worship as something unknown I am going to proclaim to you.*

**Acts 17:23**

A skilled missionary will constantly search for points of contact within the unreached people group's religion, philosophy, and/or faith that can be used as a trampoline for the message about the good Creator God who showed Himself on earth through Jesus. The missionary attempts to build a bridge between the old and the new. Many are so afraid that they will either create syncretism, a blending of religions, or begin to compromise, and in doing so deprive the cross of its power; so they dare not even try. Naturally it requires a lot of caution, discernment and sensitivity for the Spirit of God on the missionary's part. If it is possible to find an analogy (Greek, analogia =similarity, comparability), then that is an unbeatable way to show the people that God and the truth about God have been close to them all along, without them knowing. The truth has knocked on the door to the people and their culture many times before, and now it is time to open up, confess and welcome in the truth.

Paul used an extremely skillful analogy when he preached the Gospel of Jesus to the Greeks. He managed to create a bridge between their own religious practice and the revolutionizing and transforming message of salvation! The altar "to an unknown God" had been raised in remembrance of the time when the Athenians were saved from the plague by an unknown God. Everyone knew of the altar and had most likely wondered who this god might be. Paul used the legend of the altar and preached the Gospel skillfully under the anointing of the Holy Spirit to his philosophical and Hellenistic audience. Brilliant Paul!

## 6. Quote Their People of Authority, Authors, Skalds, Musicians and Icons

Paul preached that the Creator God neither lived in temples made by man nor let Himself be served by man, as if He was in need of human help. In this way, Paul showed them how close God really was to the Greeks. Paul said that all people seek God, even the Greeks, and described how they were groping around in darkness. God was much closer to the Greeks than they believed, and it was much easier to get in contact with Him than they thought.

To the intellectual and complicated Greeks, Paul's preaching was radical because of how simple it was to get to know God. In the middle of this sermon, he quickly quoted one of their own skalds:

> *'For in him we live and move and have our being... We are his offspring.'*
>
> **Acts 17:28**

With this quote from one of their own, Paul skillfully continued to explain the impossibility of God resembling something made of gold, silver or stone. The Greeks had to understand that if we are part of God's family, God will not resemble anything we humans have created through our art and fantasy. By using one of their authorities Paul nullified the whole concept of idolatry in Athens.

## 7. No Salvation Without Repentance

Paul has now reached the point of impact and challenges the people toward repentance. It does not matter how good the missionary has been in disciplining his/her spirit, building relationships, creating favor, being a Greek for the Greek, building bridges and quoting their own authorities, there will always come a time of confrontation. There is no true salvation without repentance. Some missionaries are great at the first six points on the checklist but never really get the last one. Such missionaries therefore never see any great results: true salvations and transformed lives.

Towards the end of his sermon Paul suddenly says, completely without filters and work-arounds:

> *In the past God overlooked such ignorance, but* ***now he commands all people everywhere to repent.*** *For he has set a day when he will judge the world with justice by the man he has appointed. He has given proof of this to all men by raising him from the dead.*
>
> **Acts 17:30-31 (author's emphasis)**

Paul says that God is now commanding everyone to repent and not sentence themselves to perdition in the Great Judgment one day. Repentance and true faith are connected. True faith can only be birthed in a man that has first repented.

*Therefore let us leave the elementary teachings about Christ and go on to maturity, not laying again the foundation of* ***repentance from acts that lead to death****, and of faith in God, instruction about baptisms, the laying on of hands, the resurrection of the dead, and eternal judgment*

**Hebrews 6:1-2 (author's emphasis)**

The author of Hebrews, who might very well be Paul, says that the foundations of the Christian faith are:

1. Repentance
2. Faith
3. Baptism (cleansing)
4. Baptism in the Holy Spirit (laying on of hands)

In the Book of Acts the Apostle Paul tells us about the mission God gave him when he was saved and called to ministry. He says:

*to open their eyes and* ***turn them from darkness to light, and from the power of Satan to God****, so that they may receive forgiveness of sins and a place among those who are sanctified by faith in me.*

**Acts 26:18 (author's emphasis)**

Paul had received clear instructions from God that he was to open the eyes of the unreached Gentiles in order for them to be able to repent from darkness to light and from the power of satan to God! That is salvation! In both scripture references we clearly see that repentance comes before faith.

"But then people will get mad and they will not like me and what I have to say". Yes, it is actually inevitable that people who do not want to repent will feel confronted. Truth confronts lies, light confronts darkness and the Spirit of God confronts the demons! We can read what happened after Paul had finished his speech and lecture on the Aeropagus in Athens:

> *When they heard about the resurrection of the dead, some of them sneered, but others said, "We want to hear you again on this subject." At that, Paul left the Council. A few men became followers of Paul and believed. Among them was Dionysius, a member of the Areopagus, also a woman named Damaris, and a number of others.*
>
> **Acts 17:32-34**

At the end, Paul had led four or five people to faith and they became the first disciples in Athens.

During the summer of 2004, when I was in a small Finnish town called Seinäjoki, I met a happy sixty-one-year-old Finnish man at the hamburger bar Hesburger. My good friend Krister introduced me to his dad Erkki Leimola. I knew and felt all kinds of things about Erkki in my spirit while we sat there eating. I knew that he was battling periodic alcoholism and other things, but I disciplined my spirit.

Erkki was not a Christian and I so wanted to win him to Jesus. Erkki had worked in an industry in Sweden for over twenty years and spoke good Swedish. I tried to build as much confidence as possible and it did not take long before Erkki had thawed and laughed at almost all my jokes.

My best friend the Holy Spirit whispered in my ear that I should continue to joke and laugh with Erkki. Humor happened to be one of the keys that opened up Erkki's heart for Jesus. After an hour of fellowship filled with jokes and laughter, I suddenly knew that I had gained Erkki's favor. He showed curiosity towards my Christian faith and I begin to share missionary stories.

Throughout our conversation I continued to speak "blue collar Swedish" and became a Greek for the Greek, or a Finn for the Finnish – whichever you want. Erkki was very smart and productive and had at the time a small photography shop in town. Both Erkki and I had working class backgrounds and the conversation continued at that level even though, as time passed, it became more and more focused on signs and wonders.

Suddenly I saw a vision inside my head, so to speak. I saw myself standing in a pond later that same day baptizing Erkki. It was late afternoon at Hesburger where we were sitting laughing and talking.

Erkki laughed so hard at one of my jokes that he began to cry. He exclaimed," You are a funny priest, you!"

That is when I saw the vision flash before my eyes. Without hesitating, I asked Erkki if he believed in God.

"I think I do," he answered.

"Do you believe that He became human in Jesus and died for your sins on the cross?"

"Why... if you are to believe in the God of the Bible then I suppose you need to take the entire package," Erkki responded with a smirk.

"That is probably the best," I answered with a big smile. We had reached the smash moment! It was open, I came free and glided in in-front of the goal on wobbly skates and found the goaltender had gone to the restroom. Do you get the picture? I said to Erkki:

"You are more Christian than you think, man! You are almost saved." Erkki, Christer and I all laugh together. Then I said: "I am going to baptize you this evening, Erkki!"

"Are you?" He responded.

"Yes, in some sort of pond or lake, God has shown it to me; I saw it inside my head as we were talking."

No one laughed anymore... Erkki looked at me astonished.

I said, "It is time now! It is time to repent now, Erkki! It is time to be saved now!"

Erkki nodded with tears in his eyes.

"It is not every day that you meet your priest, so let's make it a night," I said, laughing again.

Everything was set, so to speak; the Holy Spirit was at work. I did not quote any Finnish authorities or icons, there was no need. Erkki repented and true, genuine faith was born at the hamburger bar.

I continued: "Go home and get an extra pair of boxer shorts and a towel and meet me outside my hotel in half an hour. We are going to baptize you! Okay?"

"Yeah, Okay," both Erkki and Krister answered simultaneously. They dropped me off at my hotel and I ran up to my room and gathered some clothes and a towel. As I prayed I saw yet another vision. I saw Erkki wildly debating with his flatmate and her strongly dissuading him from going with a priest and getting baptized. "Are you out of your mind, Erkki?"

I called Krister on his cell and he handed the phone to his dad, who by now had started to doubt this quick baptism.

"Quick baptism?" I replied. "You have waited too long already; you are sixty-one, man! We will not wait another day, Erkki! Grab a pair of boxers and a towel and come at once!"

"Yes, let's do that," Erkki replied and, as he tossed the phone back to Krister, I heard him say: "That is one stubborn priest!" Krister laughed and hung up. Krister had prayed for his dad's salvation for a long time, this was a big day!

I met Krister and Erkki outside my hotel, and I jumped in the back of Erkki's car. "Now let us go to a lake," I said and leaned forward between the seats. As we drove around searching for a place for baptism, I read about salvation and baptism in the Bible, hanging between the seats.

We found a blasted pond next to a power station. We walked out into the water and first we prayed a prayer of salvation. I then baptized Erkki to Christ upon his own confession of faith in Jesus in the name of the Father, the Son and the Holy Spirit.

As we made our way towards the shore where Krister stood laughing, shouting congratulations to his dad, a frightened Finn out for an evening walk with his Rottweiler passed by. Erkki exclaimed: "Is this when you say Halleluljah?"

"Yes that would be appropriate now," I replied. "The right place for a Halleluljah!" (It is Hallelujah and not Halleluljah, but Erkki had not learned that yet...)

Krister took a photo! We clapped Erkki encouragingly on the back. Life was great! As we had now buried at least forty years of old trash and a pretty impressive corpse, we laughed and continued talking as we changed clothes in the sunset.

That evening Erkki, Krister and I sat talking and reading the Bible together for a long time in the car at the hotel parking lot. Just saved, with a towel around his waist, hair still wet and barefoot in his summer shoes, Erkki received the baptism in the Holy Spirit in the car. With his hands grasping the wheel, Erkki received the power and began to speak in new tongues for the first time in his life. It was a Finnish summer night at its best.

I had the great privilege to wed Erkki and his flat mate in the late summer of 2005 and we ate the wedding dinner at the ale-house behind the racetrack in Seinäjoki. Erkki is now a regular attendee at the Pentecostal church in Seinäjoki. He is one of the happiest, funniest and quickest baptized Pentecostals in Eastern Bothnia! His record still stands, I promise!

CHAPTER 5

# Street Preaching

*Jesus went through all the towns and villages, teaching in their synagogues, preaching the good news of the kingdom and healing every disease and sickness.*

**Matthew 9:35**

As European and American Christians we need to re-conquer the act of street preaching. To preach on buses, trains, city squares, metro and rail stations and in malls is something that we need to do at a much higher rate. The street preacher needs to become a common sight and just as much a natural part of street life as the juggler, street musician or the magician, which all are common on the downtown streets of Europe and America. The Christian Cultural Revolution is already here!

*Those who had been scattered preached the word wherever they went. Philip went down to a city in Samaria and proclaimed the Christ there.*

**Acts 8:4-5**

You can easily have a large crowd gather around you on the street if you dare to be professional and give it all you have. No one leaves when it is time for the preacher to step up after the dancers, actors and musicians have captured the crowd, if you learn to do it the right way. When you want to preach the Gospel briefly and give an altar call in the midst of a Christian street show filled with street theater, dances, acrobatics and a band performing, then here is some practical pices of advice to the preacher:

## 1. Force Your Audience To Listen

Keep the music playing as a backdrop or have someone sing in a whisper, accompanied by the band behind you. Do not allow yourself long pauses; make sure that something happens throughout your sermon. Wear something funny on your head such as a hat, a plastic bag, a bright red hat or something ugly and noticeable. Remember to act out your message with vivid and warm body language and captivating mimic. Sound like a circus director or DJ. Be self-secure and own the street or city square. Throw some firecrackers in the air if you have to! Sit on someone's shoulders and preach! Force your audience to listen!

## 2. Have Something In Your Hand

It makes such a difference if you have something in your hand that you eagerly want to show your audience. You can preach with a hundred dollar bill in your hand. You can wear binoculars around your neck that you at times pick up to view and study the mimics of your audience.

Joke around with the audience. You can say things like, "I can very well see the pimple on your cheek that you have gone through so much trouble to hide with makeup," or "I can see the wart that this pretty blond girl has on her nose," and so on.

Have something in your hand that you bought on a trip to Asia and that the audience has no clue about. Explain and talk about it while you preach. Everything that you choose to have in your hand will double as a parable for your message.

Let someone from the audience, a kid perhaps, hold your mic as you retrieve something from your inner pocket or from your shoe, all while you continue talking. Buy or borrow a parrot, monkey or iguana that you can have on your shoulder as you preach! Have a rabbit or Boxer dog under your arm! Talk about your friendship and how they trust you and compare this to faith. Use a RC car and drive it through your audience, juggle as you preach, paint graffiti or use a sketch board!

## 3. Illustrate and Dramatize Your Sermon

Why not use a bunch of dressed up, made over actors that dramatize as you preach. Use as many props, colors and creativity as you can! Let it explode. Use sound effects; let someone make sound effects in a mic as you preach. Use your audience for walk-on parts in the dramatization. Illustrated sermons on the streets or city squares are unbeatable!

### 4. Always Preach for Something, Never Against

There is nothing that turns off people more than an angry and confronting street preacher that seems to be against everything and everyone. Such a preacher would actually be better off leading a demonstration or a political rally. To shout out that the world is going to hell and that the poor audience is disgusting because they remain in their sin and impurity is neither attractive nor winning. You will never win a Muslim by proclaiming that Muhammed is dead and that the Quran urges the mass slaughter of Christians and Jews. You will not win a Hindu if you say that Krishna was a pervert and that Ganesha looks like a freak. Do not preach against. Do not scold your audience! Preach for! Smile, laugh and be positive! Preach Jesus!

### 5. Preach a Maximum of Ten Minutes, Preferably Three Minutes

It is possible to practice at home to learn how to compress and say a whole lot in a short time frame. There is no need to always be spontaneous and to shoot from the hip, instead you can be to the point if you take your task seriously and really prepare yourself.

## 6. Make Your Altar Call Quick and Uncomplicated

Everyone in your audience does not have to close their eyes and then raise their hands. Instead, ask, "did you like this?! How many of you would like to be in contact with a God like this 24/7?! Wave at me if you think this was good news or if you want God on your side in life!" If you have had great contact with your audience all the way through, then you will succeed with your altar call as well.

Do not make long pauses; do not get all tight and weird. Be blunt, be clear and make an ordered and encouraging altar call filled with lots of love that no one can miss out on. Make your altar call quick and without frills and then let them run and greet you! Be warm and spontaneous with the ones that respond. When they have waved to you as a response to your question and they want their sins forgiven and to have eternity with God, then simply say, "Come here then and let me pray with you!"

If there are many of you out preaching, spread out before the sermon and then help people to respond and to come to the front for a salvation prayer. You might want to have different stations set up if the audience is large. I have held spontaneous street meetings around Europe that have grown to between 800 and 1,500 people. Street meetings with crowds like this demand that the preacher stands elevated so that everyone can see him.

I have actually had a spontaneous street meeting in Ethiopia that gathered approximately 5,000 people; it was so much fun and around 300 responded to the altar call. But without the help of a stage, platform, bus roof, trailer bed or something similar, one can probably gather a maximum of 100-200 people in a semi circle.

This is so much fun! Once you have begun, you cannot stop! It becomes a way of life, a passion, something that grows and evolves continually... Good Luck!

# PART 2

I would now like to hand over the pen to a few of my co-workers in Mission SOS. In the following chapter Daniel Elvelyck and Jonatan Kvist, who both have preached on the streets of Stockholm, will share their experiences and give examples on practical, friendly, relevant, joyful, contagious evangelism!

The writer's pen is then handed over to Julia Willkander, Anna Kvist and Maria Evermin, who will show how music, dance and drama can be used to etch Jesus into the minds of the people.

Our festival coordinator, Peter Almqvist, will then take us to an ocean of salvation and healing, taking us behind the scenes on a Signs & Wonders festival among the unreached peoples of the world!

CHAPTER 6

By Daniel Elvelyck and Jonatan Kvist

# PRIEST IN ACTION

## 12 WAYS TO EVANGELIZE YOUR COMMUNITY

After some brainstorming we have tried to pick out twelve completely different methods that you can use in order to get started with modern, well-tried and good evangelism. We are no experts in this field, but we are learning new things every week. It's all about having a heart that constantly and in every situation bubbles over with Jesus!

The biggest secret to good evangelism is to listen to the Holy Spirit, but it is also important to really think how a non-believer thinks. Today there are not many outside the church who are interested in listening to Christians speaking Christianese when they try to talk about God. If Sergio and Kevin really want to stop and listen to the Gospel, we need to be folksy. The Gospel will not become unholy just because we speak the street language of the day, instead it will break forth in all its power. Often we Christians forget what an amazing message we actually have and take for granted that people aren't interested in hearing about Jesus. The European or American really is interested in God, but a glued-on, dutifully presented testimony does not attract anyone. Be yourself, be honest and share how Jesus changed your life.

To open up a street meeting with the phrase, "We want to show that we sure can have fun in church too," is an evangelistic suicide. Why should you place yourself in the offense when you could own the street? Say instead, "At church so and so, we think that there are too few events here in this city. We thought we'd change that!" Then you will have the audience on your side and all of a sudden they think it's great that the church exists! Tell a joke, give of yourself and charm the audience. If you want to succeed in evangelizing the street, forget the old methods and think new!

After the tsunami in South East Asia in 2004, many of us from Mission SOS stood up in buses and trains and said: "Considering the catastrophe in South East Asia and the dark times that we're living in right now, it's important that we take care of each other and help one another. I work as a priest and a missionary and I want to be here for you, even if you're not used to going to church." After that introduction, we were able to share that God has a plan for them and that He wants to come with peace to every worried heart. On one of these buses one of Aftonbladet's (a Swedish tabloid) journalists sat listening, and she wrote a chronicle in the paper about it. She was deeply moved and impressed that young people dared to raise their voices and tried to be of help to someone.

Another time before a mission trip to Uganda, we took the opportunity to ask some people we met on the street if they could help us: "We are traveling to Uganda to preach to a people who have never heard about Jesus. I have written a short sermon, but I don't know if it's too complicated and it may have some church words that are hard to understand. Could I try and preach for you and receive some feedback?" There are ways to preach to everyone. Get started and try it now!

Our wish and thought with our twelve examples is not necessarily that you should use exactly the methods we write about, but rather that you would begin to think new, fresh and broader when it comes to evangelism. There are actually no methods needed – it's a lifestyle.

## Cake Evangelism

> *...better a neighbor nearby than a brother far away.*
>
> **Proverbs 27:10b**

> *A gift opens the way for the giver and ushers him into the presence of the great.*
>
> **Proverbs 18:16**

**Goal:** To break with fear of man and in a natural way get to know and witness to your neighbors.

The home is a special place. It's a place where we like to spend a lot of time. If we're not at work, we enjoy being at home. It's a place where we feel secure and comfortable and relaxed, a place where we are on top of things. In other words, it's a good place for people to hear the Gospel. Every year we have new students that attend SOS Mission Bible College in Stockholm, Sweden. This is something that we take advantage of in evangelism. What better opportunity is there to visit neighbors and get to know people than when you have just moved to a new area?

To make it easier for a nervous student to visit the new neighbors and even sit down and talk for a while, cake evangelism is a great means of help. The way into many people's hearts and especially that of the man, is, as you well know, through the stomach. Therefore we give the students an assignment to bake a cake! And with the cake in his hand, the student then has to walk over, knock on the door and spontaneously present himself.

For example, he might say, "Hi! My name is Jonatan and I've recently moved into the apartment next door. I don't know anyone in the area and I thought it would be fun to visit you and bring a cake."

When the student sits at the table, he always gets an opportunity to share about God and that Jesus is the reason for him moving to Stockholm to attend a missionary training center.

The question that naturally follows is whether or not the neighbor believes in God.

Does this really work? Absolutely! Breaking the traditional and natural way to behave by instead visiting the neighbor with a cake will end up creating a nice time of fellowship over a cup of coffee. That moment will then give you many natural opportunities to share your faith.

A cake is something festive and will make most people who open the door welcome you in; but don't give up if the door closes, continue to the next neighbor instead.

You don't have to have moved into a new area recently in order to do this. Maybe there's a family that just moved in next door who needs a warm welcome and who needs to hear that Jesus still heals the sick. Even if you've lived next door to the Smith family for 15 years, it's time for them to be treated with a cake, so seize the opportunity to share how you met God.

**Remember!**

- Do it with a smile
- Think through beforehand what you will share and how to do it. Be personal.
- Don't force a situation where you tell them you believe in Jesus, but listen and take the opportunity when it comes.

## Street Meeting

*Go out quickly into the streets and alleys of the town and bring in the poor, the crippled, the blind and the lame.*

**Luke 14:21b**

**Goal:** To proclaim the Gospel, so that people will become saved everywhere in your city, on the streets and in the market places.

A few decades ago it was completely natural to find people, whether individually or in groups, preaching outside the grocery store, at the open market places or on each and every street corner. For different reasons, most Christians lost faith in these street meetings and today street meetings in most places are a very rare sight. It's time for us to change that!

Naturally very few Europeans or Americans find it interesting to listen to someone playing the guitar outside Wal-Mart or the local grocery store. What worked well fifty to sixty years ago isn't the best way to evangelize today. There's nothing wrong with the message, it's still as attractive and up-to-date as it was 2000 years ago. It's rather the form and method that need to be modernized.

In Mission SOS we have always believed in street meetings, and we have tried to use it as a tool to reach our neighbors and cities with the Gospel. Today we have street meetings almost every other week in Stockholm. Street meetings are also a common sight at our mission bases. And it works!

In some places we pray with three to salvation, somewhere else with fifteen, on a third place one person and so on. Every person that is won to Jesus causes a great feast in heaven! So how do we do this? And how can you do the same?

Be creative! Ask God for an idea that will catch people's attention. Figure out something exciting, something unusual or something that's attractive. It can be anything from break dance, blowing fire, street theater or having a skilled musician play or sing something beautiful at a city square or market place. All of Sweden loves the famous singer, Per Gessle. Sing, for example, one of his old songs. You can come up with a lot of ideas! Read about the Salvation Army and what they did at the end of the 1800's! They were extremely creative, folksy and exciting and people were saved by the droves on the streets.

When you have the attention of the people, it is time to briefly present the Gospel. No one who goes about their everyday stressful life will stay and listen to you for a long period of time. Practice how you can recap the Gospel in five minutes in a relevant way; preferably illustrating what you're talking about at the same time (use extras or actors, something that you hold in your hand, some kind of material that you are using etc).

One time I jumped up on the shoulders of a guy and sat there while I was preaching. Everyone stopped to watch and listen to what was going on. Another time I preached at one of the most central squares in Stockholm with a paper bag on my head! I promise you that there was a big crowd that stopped to listen, and tourists took pictures! A third time I had a camera in my hand and I asked everyone to step forward because I wanted to get them in the picture. All the young people rushed forward! I took a picture and then I preached for five minutes with the camera in my hand. Everyone stood quietly and many were saved.

When you've finished, pose a simple but clear question asking if someone wants to be saved, and pull in the net with newly caught fish. Maybe you'll be surprised that people in your city are being saved on the streets, but I promise it works if we only do it right.

**Remember!**

- If you plan to gather a large crowd, have a good sound system.

- Speak everyday language, not church language in order for people to understand
- Be relevant, but do not compromise the heart of the message

## 2x2 Cards

*...and, with prayer and fasting, committed them to the Lord...*

**Acts 14:23b**

**Goal:** To pray with your friend to salvation after strategic and committed preparations.

Here we'll give you a short and simple idea that is guaranteed to produce some kind of result. Actively praying and fasting for a non-Christian friend, neighbor or relative is absolutely the best way to prepare that person's heart for the Gospel. When you do this, be thorough and strategic.

Take some thick paper and cut out a piece the size of half a postcard, write down the names of two non-Christian people that you know. Then take the next two months and actively pray two minutes every day for the people on your card. Pray that they would understand the Gospel, that their hearts would be softened and that you would get an opportunity to share Jesus with them. Sometime during these two months, take two days to fast for their salvation. When the two months are over, make sure you meet with your friends. Invite them for dinner, go to a hockey game, rent a movie together, or do something that is fun. Your goal for that day is to share Jesus. Believe that the Spirit of God has worked on them for two months; be prepared to lead them to salvation right then and there!

**Remember!**

- Place the card somewhere where you won't forget it, a place where you will see it every day: in your calendar, in your Bible or on your fridge.
- When you go through your two months, don't shuffle it off, but be serious and meticulous.
- It's better not to meet both friends at the same time during the same evening. It's probably easier for them to open up to you if there's only the two of you there.

## Parties

*Then Levi held a great banquet for Jesus at his house, and a large crowd of tax collectors and others were eating with them. But the Pharisees and the teachers of the law who belonged to their sect complained to his disciples, "Why do you eat and drink with tax collectors and 'sinners'?" Jesus answered them, "It is not the healthy who need a doctor, but the sick.*

**Luke 5:29-31**

**Goal:** To reach a specifically targeted group in a relevant and fun way.

Every week there are parties held in our country. Sometimes there is a lot to celebrate and sometimes just a little. Regardless of the reason most people like to go out and enjoy an evening. Sadly, most of the time these parties end up worse than when they started. Many wake up with a hangover, not really remembering what happened the night before. So why not use one of these nights for the purpose of the Gospel and allow the guests to meet with God and remember a night when their lives took a turn? If you want to reach out to a larger group of people, then parties are a great tool to use. At a party, people are in a good mood, they feel secure and in a neutral and safe place. They do not think that Jesus actually belongs outside the church as well and will therefore not expect to have the Gospel explained to them. Parties are a goldmine!

First, seek God and ask the question, "What works in my area?" There are many different ways to throw a party and there is no general rule for what works well. That's why it's important to adjust to what will work in your surroundings. Something that works very well and what we've used several times in Stockholm are cultural parties. For example, we rent one of the school cafeterias and begin to invite people to an evening program. With posters in every hallway and on every bulletin board and flyers that are handed out, we sell the event the week before. We also challenge Christian friends to invite their non-Christian friends.

Second, plan the evening. What do you want to accomplish and how do you get there? Choose two emcees that will be responsible to create a good mood during the evening. These two will have to put themselves in the place of the guest, thinking how the audience thinks. It is their job to determine what they would appreciate and like and plan accordingly. Some examples might be; live performances, ring dances, games and so on. During our latest cultural party, one emcee was dressed in a Scandinavian folk dress while the other wore a long Arabic gown. The two of them then charmed the audience with everything from a pop quiz to a national anthem medley. With good emcees on the stage, the hearts of the guests are prepared.

It is great to present the Gospel after hours of laughter and good food. Prepare a natural transition to a more serious part of the party. Have someone share about a miracle or show a drama about Jesus. Then preach a relevant message. Remember that you are not in church, you are speaking to unbelievers; choose the right language for the right occasion.

It is not awkward to preach during a party if you plan and prepare well. To preach about the creator God who unites us human beings is perfect at a party that is held in the suburbs.

Adapt your ideas for the area where you live. For example, you don't have to rent a facility and invite strangers. It's perfectly fine to throw a taco party for your colleagues or the parent group at your son's school. Adjust the evening to your situation. It can be difficult to stand up and preach in your living room for five friends, so instead prepare yourself to share why you're a believer. This will make a big impact. End by offering to pray for them.

**Remember!**

- Plan ahead.
- If you're going to serve food, don't forget to adjust to other cultures: halal, kosher, etc.
- Prepare your sermon well.

## Interview Evangelism

*But you will receive power when the Holy Spirit comes on you; and you will be my witnesses in Jerusalem, and in all Judea and Samaria, and to the ends of the earth.*

**Acts 1:8**

**Goal:** To witness in a new way

We Christians have a very clear assignment from God. We are all called to be witnesses. Regardless of whether you are new in your faith or grew up in Sunday school, your assignment is to share Jesus. Neighbors, family, colleagues, and the cashier at the grocery store all have the right to hear about Jesus through you. You can actually be an active part of God's plan of salvation.

Even though you may feel nervous and anxious about witnessing, there are still many ways to be successful. A way that is preferable, especially if you are to evangelize to a stranger downtown, is interview evangelism. This will make both the stranger and yourself comfortable. Put together a paper with ten questions about Christianity, for example: "What do you think of when you hear the words faith, God and healing?" Add questions like, "What do you know about Jesus?" and "What would make you believe?" Take a piece of paper and a pen and hit the streets.

Make contact with a person who seems to have time and ask, "Excuse me, I'm a Christian and I'm doing some research about spirituality. Could I ask you some questions?" Most people will answer, "Yes," and you will have the opportunity to testify about Jesus.

A couple of months ago I brought my questions and rode the Metro in Stockholm. I met a middle-aged man who was on his way home from his job as a bus driver. I asked if I could ask some questions. This became an awesome opportunity. I asked one question, he answered what he thought and then I continued to share what the Bible says or what I had experienced myself. After having traveled for some time, it was time for him to get off at his station and then I finished by telling him how he could establish a relationship with God.

Interview evangelism is a great way to witness. Do not only ask the questions but seize the opportunity to testify. If you ask something about healing, tell them that God can heal today. Ask if you can pray for the person. God is not limited, so create opportunities for God to manifest His power and believe that He will work through you!

**Remember!**

- This is not a way to con people; you really want them to think with their hearts.
- Pray and prepare yourself well.
- Avoid hot topics. You will not win anything with a debate!

## Hobby Evangelism

> *...and because he was a tentmaker as they were, he stayed and worked with them.*
>
> **Acts 18:3**

**Goal:** Start a hobby to get new friends to witness to.

I have actually never liked the sauna. It's too hot and it's hard to breathe. But one day I realized that men who are in a sauna tend to interact and talk to each other a lot, so it is a perfect place to talk about Jesus. In a sauna everyone is very open. So that is what I did. I sat in the sauna and talked to the "old men" about the adventurous life with Jesus and the Gospel. Sauna evangelism is great!

You can use this idea with something you are interested in. What do you like to do? Do you collect stamps or old American cars? Do you like photography or working out? Do not open a gym at your church, but join one. You will meet people like you and there you will have the opportunity to share Jesus!

**Remember!**

- If your attitude is: "I don't have time," then you need to re-prioritize. We need to take time to reach unbelievers.
- Do not join the local stamp collector's society pretending that you like stamps if you actually do not. Use something you are genuinely interested in.
- If you try sauna evangelism, begin talking about Jesus as quickly as possible, since it is hard to sit and chat for several hours in a sauna.

## Set up a Show at Your School Auditorium

*Do not say, 'I am only a child.' You must go to everyone I send you to and say whatever I command you.*

**Jeremiah 1:7**

**Goal:** Jesus should be well known at your school!

The Swedish and American schools are actively stepping away from the Christian faith; the school is supposed to be neutral ground for the students. That is why it is more important than ever that we as Christians take our responsibility for the generation in school, especially if you yourself are still in school. Most people that are being saved today are under the age of 21.

To arrange a show in your school auditorium is both fun and challenging. For the most part it is fun, since you will be praying with your fellow students to salvation! By an auditorium show I mean that you, together with some Christian friends, should present Jesus to a larger gathering of students, so it does not necessarily have to be in an auditorium. Make sure that you plan ahead. You need to have time for all the preparations to maximize the occasion. Set a date, around Christmas or Easter, for example, and talk to the principal, explaining that you would like to set up a show that shares the message about Christmas.

Explain what the show will look like and that you have practiced songs, dance moves and dramas to make a nice show for the school. Even though the principal probably will be impressed with your ambitions, it might be difficult to make the show mandatory and use in-class-time for the show. Don't be discouraged; continue to work according to the prerequisites. Find a slot when most classes are having recess and begin to advertise the show on bulletin boards and invite as many as possible. Spread the word so that no one will miss the show! Have a runsheet so the show will flow smoothly. Alternate between break dance and testimonies, between human videos and music. Make sure this is something worth watching. When the day arrives, see to it that everyone involved knows their part and performs wholeheartedly. Be proud and testify boldly! Make it easy for the visitors to understand the Gospel!

An auditorium show can be performed in many different ways. Sometimes it is 30 minutes long, other times 10 minutes. Sometimes you are able to do almost anything you want and other times not. One time in Norway, we were permitted to dance and sing in the school cafeteria and invite people to the festival meetings in the evening, but we were not allowed to preach. On the other hand, if the students wanted to hear us, we were allowed to preach in a separate room. Naturally we seized that opportunity!

**Remember!**

- Have permission or clearance from your principal.
- Use yourself as an advertisement.
- Make sure that the message is relevant.

## Movie Night

*Do not forsake your friend...*

**Proverbs 27:10a**

**Goal:** To begin to testify to your friends.

Too often we take our friends for granted. We do not think that they would want to hear how we were saved, because if they really wanted to hear the Gospel, they would ask about it, right? No, that is not te case. Of course you show with your life that you are a Christian, but your friends will not be saved unless you open your mouth. Faith comes by hearing! Faith comes when you preach about Jesus.

That is why movie nights are so good! It is a good reason to meet with your friend and a great way to start up a natural conversation about Jesus; you are creating an opportunity to speak about things deeper than football. That is why you should choose a movie that talks about faith, life and death or something else that can be related to the Christian faith. Some examples of good movies are The Passion of the Christ, The End of the Spear, The Chronicles of Narnia or Schindler's List. After the movie, take the opportunity to share why you are saved and explain that God actually wants to get to know them too!

**Remember!**

- Choose a good movie.
- Refer back to the movie when you testify.
- Be personal.

## Music Contest

*My heart is steadfast, O God; I will sing and make music with all my soul.*

**Psalm 108:1**

**Goal:** To arrange a Jesus-filled music event for the community where you live!

Music is an important ingredient in every culture and we humans love it. Many people even build their whole identity around a certain style of music. Sometimes you can see immediately which band a person listens to just by looking at their hairdo. Shouldn't we honor God, the one who invented music (even if much of it has been perverted), by evangelizing through it?

A good way to do this is by arranging a music contest. Fill a church or another facility with visitors and give local bands the opportunity to play. You will earn great appreciation from the community and also create an opening to preach. Keep in mind that a music contest is quite a large project to arrange. You'll need a good facility, sound and preferably lighting as well. Many churches are perfect for this purpose, and probably the only thing you will need to do is remove benches and chairs.

Make sure that you have a skilled sound technician since the success of the event depends on him. Then begin to advertise the contest. Go to rehearsal halls, schools and music associations and challenge local bands to participate. You then need to fill the facility; without an audience the contest loses its purpose. Advertise the evening in every possible place: grocery stores, schools and the local newspaper. You can even send a bulk text message, use Facebook or even Twitter encouraging people to attend. When the evening arrives, you will need a talented emcee that is able to create a lively atmosphere and guide the contest.

In order for the evening to become a success it is important that the audience enjoys themselves. Have some grills set up and a small concession stand where people can buy earplugs as well as a bite to eat.

Alternate the performances with your own input – things like dancing or juggling. When the event is nearing an end and the crowd in the facility has reached its peak, it is time to preach.

Preach passionately with power and fire! It is important that you be focused. Many times you do not need more than five minutes to explain the Gospel, so do not drag out the sermon. Instead draw the head-bangers and the pop fans to salvation. Later, while you are leading the salvation prayer in an adjoining room, the contest can be resolved and everyone will have had a great evening. Especially the newly saved!

**Remember!**

- Get help from someone who knows music.
- Make sure that you have a qualified jury for the contest. You can ask the owner of the local music store or someone in the Committee for Recreational Activities.
- Have a desirable prize as an incentive to participate.

## Pray For a Sick Person

> *News about him spread all over Syria, and people brought to him all who were ill with various diseases, those suffering severe pain, the demon-possessed, those having seizures, and the paralyzed, and he healed them.*
>
> **Matthew 4:24**

**Goal:** To lay hands on a sick non-Christian and believe God for a miracle.

In the Gospels and in the book of Acts we read about many mighty and everyday healing miracles. What is interesting to note is that the healings most often took place among the people, not in the church! God wants to confirm His word and help people who are sick; we must become better at allowing Him to do that!

The Spirit of God moves every time we pray, especially if the prayer is for a person who does not know God. To lay hands on a non-Christian who is sick and pray for healing is therefore an amazing opportunity to be able to share the Gospel. The Spirit of God will be there when you pray! A miracle can take place and the person you pray for will have a wide-open heart for the Gospel. Always be prepared to lay hands on the sick and pray, regardless of your location, be it at McDonald's, in school or at the golf club.

**Remember!**

- God gives real promises: Lay your hands on the sick and they shall be healed! Expect answers to prayer!
- Always be prepared to pray for the sick; as long as you stay alert, there will be daily opportunities for you! Catch them!
- Do not pray long and do not focus on praying fancy prayers; believe God for immediate working power!

## Using Culture

*To the Jews I became like a Jew, to win the Jews...*
*I have become all things to all men so that by all possible means I might save some.*

**1 Corinthians 9:20a, 22b**

**Goal:** To use your culture to get to know non-Christians and witness to them.

Sweden is fantastic! We have so many beautiful and good things in our culture that we Swedes love to do. Just think about it, when we have our national song contest, "schlager-SM," our entire country has contest fever and everyone nervously follows Carola, Kicki, Tommy Nilsson and other famous contestants. And we must not forget to mention the World Cup in soccer, the summer Olympic Games, or the European athletics championships. During these events, our entire country cries for joy when Carolina Kluft wins yet again, or screams when Zlatan Ibrahimowic scores in soccer. We gather as Swedes and rejoice and suffer together.

So what do we Christians do? Well, many meet their best Christian friends and watch soccer or the national song contest on TV. You have a nice and safe evening together. How boring! I've realized that it's during the World Cup in soccer that I need to be at the local sports bar with a Coke in my hand, cheering and screaming with all the other Swedes. It's so easy to connect with people there! I get to know new people that I can exchange phone numbers with. There I can share Jesus with my newly found friend in the late evening hours. There I can lay my hands on the sick and practice the Gospel.

It does not matter where in the world you live, use points of contact from your own culture. For example, if you live in the United States, both Thanksgiving and the Super Bowl are great opportunities. Instead of inviting your best Christian friends to watch the next Super Bowl game at your house, invite your neighbors and have a fun evening together. Invite an immigrant family for Thanksgiving Dinner next year and teach them American traditions and at the same time, fill them with the Gospel! Gather some friends from the church and practice a skit that explains the Gospel and find a large bonfire in town and perform it there. This is where people are. This is where it's easy to make new friends. This is where the Gospel fits perfectly!

**Remember!**

- You do not have to view every person in the sports bar as a salvation object. Have fun! Be natural and make new friends and make sure that your heart bubbles over with Jesus!
- Do not reject everything in a cultural festival only because there might be some shady things involved. Be a Swede to win the Swede, American to win the American, etc.
- Be prepared to answer when somebody asks you about Jesus and try to lead the conversation in that direction.

## Sports Evangelism

*Therefore I do not run like a man running aimlessly; I do not fight like a man beating the air.*

**1 Corinthians 9:26**

**Goal:** To pray with people to salvation during sports events.

Swedes are good at sports and athletics. Just think how our small country with nine million inhabitants has managed to produce stars in every kind of sport. The reason is probably because the world of sports is our absolutely widest movement today; in almost every family there is someone who is practicing some sport. That is why we need to use this platform to preach Jesus!

Through the years during our outreaches we have noticed that we have prayed with most people to salvation when we have done something related to sports. We have had basketball and soccer tournaments, floor hockey events and so on. These types of events gather a lot of people, especially young people and also a whole lot of immigrants.

Basically it is about doing the same thing regardless of the sport. Print nice posters and put them in schools, different communities, suburbs and apartment houses about two weeks before the event. Have the teams sign up and then get started. Be professional! Be well prepared; do it nicely and thoroughly. Preferably have a small concession stand where the contestants are able to buy candy, hot dogs or sandwiches, and then they will not have to go anywhere else.

It is important that the tournament be set up in such a way that all the teams can participate for as long as possible. No one should have to quit after half time, because then they'll just shower and go home! No, let the teams stay in the tournament for a long time. Then, just before the playoff (or, even better, the final, when everyone will be excited and expectant, because they will want to know who is going to win) perform a cool show. Plan for a dance, drama, beat box, or something else that will rock the house. After this someone will preach a simple and short message about Jesus! I promise, if you are bold and if you are able to capture a teenage audience and make them listen, many will be saved!

During a basketball tournament that we had a couple of years ago, we put up large speakers that were blaring hip-hop music. We had graffiti painting and a dance show and then our dear friend Walter Zuniga preached. In broken immigrant Swedish he managed to win the respect of the whole suburban gang of about 70 people. That evening most of the people in the audience decided to pray a salvation prayer before the final was played. It was a very successful sports event!

**Remember!**

- If you are going to arrange a sports event, be thorough! Young people are picky but if it is well done they will want to participate again.
- Use qualified referees in order to avoid any fights.
- Mingle with the audience, have a hot dog with a the teenagers and win their hearts.

## CHAPTER 7

By Julia Willkander, Anna Kvist and Maria Evermin

# USE YOUR CREATIVE GIFT

During the last seven years Mission SOS has developed a strong team which specializes in getting the Gospel out in different and creative ways, using song, dance and drama. In our festivals and outreaches all over the world the creative team is there, demonstrating the Gospel with the help of their gifts. It is an amazing asset in evangelism; you can preach straight into a person's life and situation in more ways than when an ordinary sermon is preached. It can be done through the lyrics of a song, a vivid drama or a dance that describes the Christian message; there are many different ways to say the same thing. We have discovered that some people find it hard to receive the words from a preacher because of prejudice, so we present the Word of God in a different way, regardless of what people think about priests and churches. A skater downtown may not want to listen to "church-talk," but when the Gospel is presented through a break dance, he will listen! God has a way to reach every person.

Presenting God in a creative way is a key to reaching beyond people's walls and their pre-conceived ideas. The creative team is like a plow that makes a way where there is not one. It is necessary to soften the earth before you can sow, and we want the seed (the message) to fall into good ground. In order for this to happen, we, the creative team, cooperate with the preacher and help him/her to get the audience going and soften them up so that he/she is able to reach out with the message immediately.

Before every festival we pray and fast, asking God what He wants to say through our creative gifts, specifically to the people we are going to visit. We create our own material and customize the repertory in order for it to be relevant to different countries and cultures. It is important to note that there is a difference between songs, dances and dramas that are simply penned down and ones that are born in prayer. It's the latter category that will reach deep and touch people, because it comes straight from heaven.

Our co-workers in the music, dance and drama teams work together and have developed several performances where two or three of these different aspects are included. We have chosen to call these "multi-numbers." Our goal is to fully develop this concept of multi-faceted performances and, in the long run, present Christian shows and musicals. We are also working on all-night-events in which there is a common theme represented within all the creative elements. During the last few years we have also made use of different media in the performances to be able to show more visibly what Jesus has done on the cross.

## Be a Good Steward of Talent

In Luke 19:12-27 Jesus shares a parable about the servants who were supposed to administer their gifts. This Bible passage is very relevant in regards to the attitude in the creative office. God has given everyone unique gifts and He wants us to use them as a tool to expand His kingdom on the earth. Dare to believe that your gifts are from God and dare to trust that you are good enough. God wants to use you! But it is also important that you administer your gift well, that you fine tune it and constantly aim to develop and improve it. Practice makes perfect!

God is the God of abundance and He always wants to give us more, but He wants to know if He can trust us. He wants to see if we are ready to care for what has been given to us in a good way. If you show yourself faithful in the small things, God can trust you with bigger areas in the future. You did not receive your creative gift in order for you to be seen and to shine. It is not about you, your career and your dreams; it is about something much bigger. It is about doing the will of God. Sometimes you first have to die to your gift and give it back to God for Him to be able to use you for something big.

It is only then, when we have the right attitude towards our assignment and gift, that the anointing, the presence of God, can descend. It comes as a result of an intimate relationship with the Holy Spirit, and by being careful to live purely and by working on one's character. You can never take the anointing for granted; it is only about the grace of God. This is what touches people when we sing, dance or do a drama. You will not go far with your gift in your own strength, but everything is possible if you put it in God's hands. Trust therefore that your gift is from God, be a good steward and be bold. You and God make an unbeatable team!

## Excellence

*Do you see a man skilled in his work? He will serve before kings; he will not serve before obscure men.*

**Proverbs 22:29**

If you're skilled in what you do, God will want to use you for great things. God loves it when we do things with excellence; that is when we are good stewards of our gift. We represent Jesus and He is worthy of the best. Don't be careless, but be particular in everything. God expects that you always do your best.

Sometimes there is lack of professional thinking in the church when it comes to creative elements, but this is not how it is supposed to be. We should be more professional than non-Christian artists because we serve a higher cause. We are not supposed to try hard to imitate the world, we should instead write new and fresh material. In the Holy Spirit we have an inexhaustible resource of inspiration that creates the most appealing element for every occasion.

## Be on Your Guard

People who stand in the spotlight are often at a higher risk of falling, i.e. for pride.

> *Pride goes before destruction, a haughty spirit before a fall.*
>
> **Proverbs 16:18**

The devil is a good example of this. He was skilled and wanted to receive the glory for what God had given him and that became his downfall. For example, it is easy to become prideful when people are applauding you because you sang or danced well, but be on your guard and give the glory to God. If we have the fear of God and walk with God, it is easier to maintain a humble heart and keep us from falling into pride or other sin.

> *Therefore, my brothers, be all the more eager to make your calling and election sure. For if you do these things, you will never fall...*
>
> **2 Peter 1:10**

We must always remind ourselves that God is the one who has placed us where we are, and we can do nothing without Him. It is easy to believe that everything is up to us, but it is only the grace of God that He uses us humans as His tools. This is something we should never forget. Remind yourself of where you came from and who you were, or what you did before God stepped into the picture.

God's love is what drives us in what we do for the kingdom. When you begin to pray and fast for your context, city or different people groups you will begin to feel the heartbeat of God, His compassion and zeal for these people. When you love the people with the love of God it will shine through everything you say and do (1 Corinthians 13:1-7). It will also drive you to try, in every way possible, to reach them with the Gospel. What is in your heart is also what you give to everyone, everywhere you go. Make sure that Jesus is the one who is seen and not you!

## Song and Music

By Julia Willkander

I grew up with song and music and began to perform and sing for people when I was three years old, holding concerts where I had the opportunity to minister with song. During the last seven years I have also been entrusted with starting and leading the music department in Mission SOS, which has given me experience in using song and music as a tool in evangelism. During the same time I have also been responsible for all the worship at SOS Mission Bible College in Stockholm. Because of this I now have some experience in using music and singing as a part of evangelism.

Song and music have a special ability to reach deep within people. Music has the power to penetrate straight into people's hearts and play on the sensitive strings of the soul; it can have a healing effect or it can be destructive, pulling people down. Through all generations, people have, regardless of language or culture, used song and music as a way of expression to convey a message or feeling. Music has the power to affect us both consciously and subconsciously.

The Bible is, to say the least, full of verses that talk about song and music, both in the New and Old Testament and this has always played a significant role in church services for Christians all over the world. Song and music are uplifting for us human beings, for our spirits, souls and bodies. The Bible encourages us to use music as a tool to minister to one another, but first and foremost to honor God.

> *Let the word of Christ dwell in you richly as you teach and admonish one another with all wisdom, and as you sing psalms, hymns and spiritual songs with gratitude in your hearts to God.*
>
> **Colossians 3:16**

> *Sing to God, sing praise to his name, extol him who rides on the clouds, his name is the LORD—and rejoice before him.*
>
> **Psalms 68:4**

## The Difference Between Performance and Worship

Most Christians know what worship is. There are several books written on the subject, so I have chosen not to dig into that in this book. Christian performance, on the other hand, is a new concept for many, which is why I have decided to focus on that. I have heard many Christians discuss the meaning of worship music. Is worship a certain musical style, or is it a collective name for all forms of Christian music? There are different opinions about this and there is probably no definitive answer to the question, but I have chosen to divide Christian music into two categories that I call worship and performance.

**Worship: for God, with the people** Worship is directed towards God and the goal for a worship leader is to bring the people before the throne of God and make the church/audience participate in song.

I have tried to briefly describe what worship is to me:

- Worship is a lifestyle.
- Worship is a way to fellowship with God, through praise and prayer.
- Worship is a natural part of an intimate life with the Holy Spirit.
- Worship is about focusing on Jesus and what He has done for us on the cross.
- Worship is not about you and what you can get, it is about giving to God.
- Worship is a way for us to enter the most holy place and simply fellowship with the living God. It is a way for us to show our love and appreciation to our Lord, Creator and Savior.

**Performance: about God, for the people** Performance means to step forward, participate, to be seen and to act. It is not about you being seen for your own sake, it is about us as singers stepping forward to make Jesus seen. The entire purpose for your performance is to minister to others with your creative gift.

A Christian performance song is not always directed towards God, but it often talks about God. When the music staff in Mission SOS has an outreach in a Swedish city or are about to sing at a large festival in Africa, it is not always fitting to sing worship songs (to God, with the people). Unbelievers do not always know what worship is and will have a hard time praising and honoring a God whom they do not believe in.

> *How, then, can they call on the one they have not believed in? And how can they believe in the one of whom they have not heard? And how can they hear without someone preaching to them?*
>
> **Romans 10:14**

A Christian performance song contains a message that reaches the people. Our assignment as singers and musicians is to preach through the gift that God has given us, which is why I view myself as a singing evangelist. Many do not understand the difference between these two categories, some people may think it is wrong to sing performance songs, while others feel that worship is too cheesy. I am convinced that you can do both and do it in a way that is pleasing to God. It is important to know when to use which style; if you mix them too much it may be confusing for the listener.

**Example 1** Johanna from the church choir is supposed to sing a solo on an outreach that her church is having at the city square. She has chosen to sing a well known love song by Céline Dion because it is more relevant for unbelievers. Johanna is a skilled worship leader and is used to lifting her hands and closing her eyes during worship. Because of this, she doesn't realize that she is doing the same thing at the outreach that she would do if she were leading worship in church.

The problem in this case is that the people in the city do not understand why the girl on stage is standing with her eyes shut throughout the performance. Johanna doesn't realize that she spontaneously and unconsciously has lifted her one hand. This creates an awkward situation where people either think the performance is silly or hard to understand. It becomes an irritating distraction that takes the focus off the song that actually had strong lyrics about love.

**Example 2** David is the lead singer in a rock band that has held several concerts in different clubs in town. He is known for his charisma and for the fact that he really knows how to perform on stage. He was saved a couple of months ago and now wants to become involved in the worship ministry in the church. During one Sunday service he is one of the lead singers, and when the music begins with a fast song, he gives it all he has got. He is thinking: "Finally, I get to show the church my talent!" Sure, he will have the church rocking during the first song, but when the worship becomes more intimate, the people in the church will have a hard time focusing on the Lord. It is completely obvious that David is doing his own thing and views himself as a lead singer.

Johanna and David continued to sing the way they were used to. It is not that either worship or performance is better than the other, but there are different occasions when one fits better than the other. Every Christian should love worship. It is a gift from God to be able to express our joy and love to the Creator through song and music. To begin the day by listening to a worship CD or by singing is amazing. Since unbelievers have a hard time understanding praise and worship, we Christians must be flexible and change our style, but not our message.

The foundation for a performance song is that you are secure and mature in your relationship with God and that you are able to give the attention you receive on stage back to God. All the glory belongs to God! If you want to hold a meeting for unbelievers, it may sometimes be a better idea to sing a proclaiming performance song about the greatness of God for the audience, than to have a 20 minute worship session. That can create an unnecessary us-and-them feeling in the meeting. The Christians know the songs and sing along, while the new visitors watch from the side.

**Non-Christian Performance** In Mission SOS we also use a lot of non-Christian performance songs. The reason for choosing such songs is to catch the attention of people. It is more likely that people on the street will stop and listen to someone singing a song they recognize from the radio, than to a completely unknown song, regardless of how good the lyrics are. It is important to be careful with the lyrics in a non-Christian song; you cannot use all songs because you have to stand for every word you sing. But there are many incredibly beautiful and powerful songs about love that can be interpreted into Christian lyrics.

You can often begin an outreach with such a song and then, when people have stopped to listen, sing other songs that describe who Jesus is. The goal is to make people hear the Gospel, but it is totally okay to sing songs where the name of Jesus is not even mentioned. It is important to look at the creative program as a package that works together to clearly present the Word of God. The singing, dance and drama open up the way and make it easier for people to receive the message.

At an outreach we had at Harvest Center Church we opened up the service with Michael Jackson's Black or White (we did however change some of the words before performing). Our theme for the evening was Racism, Xenophobia and Integration. It was successful and our audience felt relaxed and at home and they had a positive attitude for the rest of the evening.

## Practical Tips for Performing on Stage

**Boldness** It is always more fun to watch someone who dares to give of himself on stage than someone who is ashamed of what he or she is doing. Dare to trust that what you do is good enough. Even though you might feel insecure on the inside, this is not something that needs to be shown or shared with the audience. Be bold and perform to the best of your ability, then

God will come to your aid and do the rest. Pray that He will help you overcome your fear of man and pray for His kind of charisma. Shine Jesus!

**Identify With the Lyrics and Stay Focused** People will listen more closely to you if they perceive that you really mean what you sing. Think of every word and identify with the lyrics. If you do that the song will be more nuanced and pleasant to listen to. You can also adjust your moves based on what the lyrics talk about. It is a challenge to keep focus and energy throughout an entire performance. Often you find yourself standing in front of an audience that does not respond at all, regardless of how much you give of yourself. At that point it is important that you do not become discouraged, but keep going and keep the focus and the energy. Finally you will notice that you have broken through and you will have the audience with you. Always remember that you have the Holy Spirit with you and He wants to help you reach the people. Think about Him when you sing, and you will get your focus right.

**How to Move on Stage** There are not many who want to watch an insecure and intimidated singer who hardly moves to the music, so dare to express your moves! If you find it hard to begin to do that, my advice is that you make sure that you keep moving your feet during the song, this will make the rest of your body sway. You can actually practice at home by singing and expressing yourself in front of a mirror, then you will see what looks good or silly.

**Microphone-technique** Do not be afraid of the microphone! It is one of your biggest means of help. Keep the microphone close to your mouth so you can hear yourself better; this also makes it easier for the sound technician to adjust the sound. You can also practice the technique of adjusting the distance between the microphone and your mouth to correspond with how loud you are singing.

**What Should You Look At?** Let your eyes span the audience and do not forget to turn to the audience on the left and right of the stage from time to time. Dare to look people in the eyes and be personal. If there are several people on stage and someone is singing a solo, it is important that you give that person your undivided attention (unless you have agreed upon something else). If you stand looking at something else, people in the audience will do the same thing and that removes the focus from the message.

**What to Do When You Go Blank on Stage?** Smile! Everyone does that from time to time. The important thing for you to remember is not to make a big deal out of it. Be calm, there is nothing wrong with a short improvised pause. If all of a sudden you forget the lyrics, sing the second verse instead, improvise new lyrics or be quiet for a second until you are back on track. People do not remember the small mistakes but instead the general impression of the performance. Do not allow a small mistake to take away your boldness; instead keep going as if nothing happened. You can even joke about it a little, but do not excuse yourself and do not become nervous, that is when people will notice what has happened.

**Outfit** If you want to increase the effect of a multi-number, clothes and make-up can make a difference in the appearance. It is important to choose clothes that suit the song that will be performed and it also looks better if thought has been put into the color combinations.

Naturally it is important to avoid wearing provocative clothes that can be perceived as offensive. Different places and cultures have different taboos regarding clothing. In one country black is associated with death, in another yellow is associated with the government, and among many Muslim people it is not okay to show knees or shoulders. In the creative department in Mission SOS we find working with a dress code to be a lot of fun, but it is important that the focus is on the right thing. Never allow the time in prayer to be shorter than the time you spend in front of the mirror!

**Start and Finish** Remember that a performance begins when you enter the stage and does not end until you have walked off. That is why both the beginning and how you thank the audience for the applause at the end are so important. Think through everything so that your whole appearance on stage is professional.

## Receiving Praise

When you have sung or played a solo, there are often many people who come to you afterwards thanking you for the performance. Do not say: "Oh, I cannot sing that well," or

"Oh well, that was nothing special." That is false humility and a typical mindset that unfortunately is prevalent in the Scandinavian countries of Europe. Instead thank them for their praise and say: "I am so glad you liked the song." Just a simple "Thank you" is sufficient as well. If someone wants to praise you, it is impolite of you to say something contrary to what they have said. You cannot decide what others will say, but you are able to control your heart.

When you receive praise, allow it to go straight to God in your heart. Remind yourself of the fact that your song/music is a gift from God and the only reason that you are able to sing before people is the grace of God. If you do that, people will feel that you are truly humble and real.

## What Songs Should Be Used?

When we are abroad, we try to learn at least one new song in the local language. That really wins the trust of the people and it can make a hard-to-please audience soften in a matter of minutes. If you choose English songs you first have to find out how much English the people in the region know. It does not matter how good the lyrics are if the people still do not understand them. If you are searching for a song to fit a specific theme and cannot find one, my suggestion is that you write your own. Dare to try writing new songs!

At a service for unbelievers it is important to think through what kind of worship songs are to be used. They have to be Jesus-centered and must have a simple distinct message that can be understood by someone who does not know much about Christianity. An unbeliever can easily misinterpret lyrics like: "Emmanuel, our God is with us" or "I want to live in your fire." They may think, "Who is Emmanuel and how is it possible for any of us to live in fire?" If you do not know that Jesus is symbolized by a lamb, then it can be very hard to digest lyrics that describe a lamb sitting on a throne that has given its blood. I am not saying that it is wrong to use symbolic words in worship songs; it can be very appropriate and powerful at a meeting with only Christians present, but try to put yourself in the perspective of an unbeliever. As a worship team we also want to be priests for those who don't go to church.

## Writing Your Own Songs

It is not always easy to find the right song for the right occasion, so that is the perfect occasion for you to create something new. Mission SOS music department is blessed with a co-worker by the name of Linnea Hagenfors. She has an amazing gift in writing beautiful, challenging and catching songs that move the heart. In the following text she shares her ideas and knowledge about how to go about writing a song:

First and foremost, what you need is inspiration; the Holy Spirit is excellent in giving this. You can write about an occasion, a feeling, something that has touched you, a subject from the Bible, a sermon, or a scripture verse. Allow your imagination to flow freely!

One way to get started is to begin to sing in tongues for a while. After a short while you might begin to distinguish a repetitive melody, this is a good start. Sing a lot in tongues, it is amazingly refreshing, quickening and fun.

A simple practice for a beginner is to write down a prayer or a short text of thanksgiving that you then attempt to sing. You can stick to just a couple of chords, that is enough! When you have received an idea, get busy. A great means of help is the recording function on your cell phone. It is an advantage if you know how to play an instrument, or you can get help from a friend who is a musician.

Some people find it easier to write lyrics to a melody, while others figure out the melody and music when the lyrics are completed, you choose what suits you best. If you want to, you can write rhymes, but it is not necessary. What is important to remember is that both verses should have about the same rhythm and melody, but different lyrics.

When you have written a lyric, you can begin to read it rhythmically or begin to hum an accompanying melody. This is when you decide what type of feeling the song should have. Try to play the song to some simple chords that fit together. To end up, you can add details to the song, such as an intro, bridge, musical theme and so on. When the song is finished, type it all on your computer and make a document including lyrics and a chord analysis. You can also write together with someone else, maybe one of you is good at lyrics and the other is good with melodies.

There are unending variations in how a song is built up, but this is what the structure of most songs looks like:

| | |
|---|---|
| **Intro** | It should capture the attention of the listener. |
| **Verse 1** | This is the base of the song, which is often held back in intensity. |
| **Chorus** | This is the climax of the song! It should pref erably reach higher tones than the verses. |
| **Verse 2** | Here you continue to share something that has to do with the rest of the song. |
| **Chorus 2** | This is the one that really sticks with the listener so he/she should be able to sing along. |
| **Bridge** | This should surprise or add something new. |
| **Chorus 3** | Give everything once or twice. |
| **Ending** | This finishes the song. |

This was only a simple and basic presentation, but if you use this, you will go far. Believe in yourself and dare to try, songwriting really is a whole lot of fun. You might not write a masterpiece at once, but do not despise the small beginnings. Try different things and do not be afraid of failure. Practice makes perfect! Good Luck!

*Linnea Hagenfors*

## The Singers Stand on the Frontline

There is something very strong in worship and music that declares the truths of God. Song and music are a form of spiritual warfare.

*After consulting the people, Jehoshaphat appointed men to sing to the LORD and to praise him for the splendor of his holiness* ***as they went out at the head of the army, saying****: "Give thanks to the LORD, for his love endures forever." As they began to sing and praise, the LORD set ambushes against the men of Ammon and Moab and Mount Seir who were invading Judah, and they were defeated.*

**2 Chronicles 20:21-22 (author's emphasis)**

This is one of the reasons to why we allow the worship or song team to start up our festival meetings. It is not only to warm up the audience, but also to punch a hole in the spiritual realm. That is why it is not unusual that the creative team and especially the singers get sudden stomach problems or sore throats just hours before a festival meeting. The devil is afraid because he knows that heavy artillery is on the way.

One time, at a festival in Ethiopia, I all of a sudden had a terrible cold, in 95° F heat! I lost my voice and it did not look like I was going to be able to sing at the festival meeting that night. But I knew this was an attack from the devil and told my team that I was going to sing at the meeting regardless. Five minutes before I was to stand on the stage I could only whisper to my music team but we prayed together and I stepped up on the platform in faith. We began singing and when it was time for my solo, I discovered that my voice was back. After another three fast songs I came down from the stage and my voice was better than it had been for many days! Since then I have faith for voice miracles.

## Singing Evangelist

Christian performance is about serving others. It is amazing to be able to sing about God's greatness and His mighty promises through one's song. We preach by singing strong-to-the-core truths about God's kingdom.

> *Sing to the LORD, praise his name; proclaim his salvation day after day. Declare his glory among the nations, his marvelous deeds among all peoples.*
>
> **Psalm 96:2-3**

A well known pedagogic trick is that if you want to remember something important you can add a melody to it. Putting music to Bible verses makes it easy to remind oneself of God's promises to us. My goal is to sing and write music for those who have never heard the Gospel before. It is a challenge to explain the Gospel in a little over three minutes without using common Christian phrases.

Before a new festival I pray and fast, and ask God what He wants me to say to this specific people group that we are going to visit. I do not play an instrument and I cannot write songs on demand, but still God has given me the grace to hear melodies and see lyrics while in prayer. I do not write songs, they are delivered to me from heaven.

Before one of our festivals in Kenya, I received the following lyrics that contain many truths about God:

*The power of God is here*
*The King is alive and rules in this place*
*The power of God is here*
*And He makes you whole in body and soul*

*If you want eternal life you have come to the right place*
*Because we describe how you can live forever from this day*
*Just believe, with all your heart, confess that Jesus lives*
*And you will feel His power when you start to praise His name*

Before a festival in Namalu, Uganda, I received a song specifically for that town. We sang the song during every meeting and, a few days into the festival, when we were out on the streets having outreaches, people began singing that song as soon as they saw us. When we were to travel back home from Namalu, the children ran beside the bus and happily sang, "Namalu, Oh, Oh, Oh, Jesus is here for you!" My eyes were filled with tears. If they do not remember anything else from that festival week, they will have the lyrics of a song that will remain with them for the rest of their lives. Jesus is there for them.

Another beautiful memory is from Lesotho where we held two festivals within only four months. My sister Linnea birthed a song in prayer for the Basotho people. They learned the song during the first festival and when we returned the second time, we only had to play the intro and the audience began to cheer. The people had taken the lyrics to heart and made it their own. When the chorus began, the whole audience of more than 8,000 people became completely wild and jumped, danced and sang out with full force: "He is the God of miracles, He is the God who heals, and nothing is impossible when He draws near." The people had received something tangible to put their faith in. That song created something in the spirit world and opened up the heavens at the festival site.

My hope is that this teaching will help you dare to take new steps and to use song and music as tools to reach out with the Gospel. I am so thankful to God that I am able to do what I love, to sing and at the same time work doing the Great Commission. I have two scripture verses that I stand on and often return to:

> *I will sing to the LORD all my life; I will sing praise to my God as long as I live.*
>
> **Psalm 104:33**

> *I am the Lord's servant, Mary answered. May it be to me as you have said.*
>
> **Luke 1:38**

I am an ordinary woman who has received a gift from God, but I have decided to be the best possible steward of that gift. I have prayed to God that He would use me and I am ready to go where He wants to lead me. I am going to continue to do what I know God has called me to do: to sing about Jesus.

# DANCE

By Anna Kvist

In Mission SOS we use dance as one of the tools in our work to reach the unreached peoples with the Gospel. Oh, if you could join us and watch how dance creates joy among our visitors on the festival site! Tens of thousands of people dancing together whipping up dust whirls, it is really an experience! Men and women from different religions and ethnicities relax when we dance, sweat and laugh side by side. We come close to one another and all of a sudden we are no longer strangers. And when prejudice, fear and hate are gone, God can work mightily!

## Dance is God's Invention

Dance as an expression is originally meant to honor and please God, but often it is connected to something provocative and seductive. It was never God's thought that dance would be connected to sin. The devil always wants to steal the beautiful things God has created in order to pervert it, but we are supposed to reclaim what was stolen. Dance was meant to be used to honor God and to preach the good news! We are to use dance to glorify Him; pure, beautiful and proclaiming dances where Jesus is in the center and we as dancers are forgotten.

## Different Types of Dances

Dance has encountered and still does encounter resistance from churches and certain Christian circles. What the critics often do not know is that dance is completely Biblical. Besides many practical ideas on how you can work with dance, I will give you a firm Biblical foundation to stand on! The Bible talks about many different types of dance; different dances are for different occasions. Below are some examples:

**Worship Dance** Worship dance is maybe the most common term for dance in the church. It is as if this title has become a common name for different types of Christian dance. It is important to highlight the actual meaning of this term. It is not about dancing for people; this is something between you and God. Just like when you sing worship songs to honor God, you can also dance to honor Him. You praise Him with your whole body and show how much you love Him and your joy over salvation.

The first time dance is mentioned in the Bible is when the people of Israel had walked out from captivity in Egypt. They had experienced one of the most spectacular miracles in the Bible: when God parted the Red Sea. In Exodus 15:20 you can read how Miriam the prophetess praised God by dancing with thanksgiving for the miracle she and the people had experienced.

In 2 Samuel 6:5-23 the story is told about King David who danced with all his might before the Lord. He had so much to praise God for that he danced on the streets of Jerusalem. This passage also tells about his wife Michal, who despised David because he danced and made a fool of himself before the people. For the consequence of her contempt, she received the shame of barrenness, which she bore for the rest of her life. So it is important to praise God and love Him more than one's own reputation and prestige. God loves it when you dance before Him!

Seven years ago I lived in the city of Jönköping, Sweden and was a member of an amazing church there. During one of the Sunday morning services I danced a worship dance before the whole congregation. It was a very beautiful dance in which I expressed the love between me and God. During my dance, God's wonderful presence and glory filled the sanctuary and many of the members in the congregation were ministered to. It was a powerful experience in which God ministered through the worship dance!

**Victory Dance** Victory dance is mentioned several times in the Bible and is about dancing with the joy of a conqueror in ecstatic victory before God. There are many in the Bible who express themselves through dance and proclaim the victory of the Lord. You will find examples of this in the book of Judges 11:34, when Jephta's daughter danced and celebrated her father's victory over the Ammonites.

In 1 Samuel 17 and 18, you can read about the young boy David who defeated the warrior giant Goliath from Gath. After this, David became the commander-in-chief over the army of Israel and succeeded in the war against the Philistines. The women danced in true celebration joy over the victory that the Lord had given them. This victory over the Philistines was an answer to prayer for the people.

It may also be good to know that Jesus, in Luke 6:23, also encouraged us to dance for joy in times of persecution. So the next time you receive an answer to prayer or go through difficult times, dance and rejoice before God. It is Biblical!

When we are out on a festival trip, there are sometimes things that work against us. It can be the mayor of a city who does not want to give us permission to have an outreach, or an African downpour. Regardless of what the circumstances look like, we always proclaim the victory of Jesus! We continue to dance a dance about the fact that Jesus reigns, even if the audience suddenly disappears to search for protection from the rain. We sing about the victory of Jesus and continue to sing even if the sound system crashes. We lift Him up under every circumstance and through Him, we are always victorious!

**Performance Dance** A performance dance, in which glorifying God is not the main purpose, is also mentioned in the Bible. You can read about it in the book of Judges 21:21. Here the women danced a performance dance. There does not have to be anything wrong with dancing in order to create an enjoyable atmosphere, but you need to be aware of why you are dancing.

The reason for this kind of dancing is that it is fun and creates a festive atmosphere, which is totally okay, as long as it is done with high standards and purity in mind. It is not a sin to use dance to make the guests laugh and relax, because even that is found in the Bible. In Stockholm we often have dance at our parties. It can be a ring dance at a wedding or a line dance at a birthday party. When we arranged a party in May 2007, we had a medley with Swedish summer songs that we danced to. The excitement in the atmosphere increased when everyone began singing and dancing together. Our purpose had been to simply make everybody feel at home and we had succeeded!

## Dance in Evangelism

Dance is Biblical and that's why we use it in evangelism. In Mission SOS we use different dances with a message, either dance for believers or dance as an evangelism tool. These different types of dance contain and describe a story or a message that we want to convey. For example, it may show the journey of a young girl looking for the meaning of life, who then meets Jesus and finds salvation, or it may show a specific feeling, like joy or hope, that can be found in Jesus.

**Dance for believers** communicates a message to people who already know Jesus. It is very good to make dances for believers, for churches or for Christian youth at conferences. These dances are encouraging and challenge believers to take new steps of faith, to go out in missions or to draw closer to Jesus!

**Dance as an evangelism** tool presents Jesus to those who do not know Him. Here the pure Gospel is preached through the dance and we can paint Jesus, who He is and what He has done.

In every dance that carries a message it is important to think about what you want to convey. When we hold our annual missions festival Harvest Cry in Stockholm, one of the festival meetings usually has missions as a theme. Then we show a dance which has the sole purpose of challenging people to begin to work actively on the Great Commandment. On the other hand, when we hold meetings for unbelievers, we feature dances that have a clear salvation message, that challenge guests to receive Jesus into their hearts.

It pays off to be specific, so adjust the dance according to the setting that you are in and to the people who will see the dance. Then the creative tools will become a common spearhead into people's lives. Starting an outreach by spreading joy to the audience through dance and then preaching about that same joy has a powerful effect. Whether we dance, act out a drama or preach, we are all pointing to the same thing.

## The First Steps

If you are making the choreography for a dance, there are a couple of things you need to think about. The first thing you need to ask yourself is: what is the purpose for this dance? Is it to challenge your Christian friends to reach the immigrant area in your city, or to present salvation for your friends at the youth center?

Determine the music, style, moves and story line based on the dance's purpose. It is important that you choose the song carefully; it needs to reinforce what you want to share.

- It is important to choose a song with a good message and strong lyrics.
- Preferably choose a song that many will recognize, or a song that is catching and makes people want to stop and look at you.

- If you are dancing abroad on a mission trip, plan to adapt the music to the culture or choose a song in their local language; that will be a winning move!

You do not have to choose a Christian song just because you are doing an evangelistic dance. There are many non-Christian songs with good lyrics. What is important is that you listen closely to the lyrics; you need to be able to stand for the entire song!

In the Western world people are often picky when it comes to what they think is good and what is not. That is why it is extra important that you choose a catchy song; preferably one that people outside the church will recognize. Many of today's non-Christian artists write songs that talk about the meaning of life or man's longing for something greater to live for. If there is a song that is constantly being played on the radio with meaningful lyrics, choose that one! That way you will make it easier for people to stop and listen to what you have to say!

When you have found a song and you know what you want to convey with the dance, begin working with the choreography. There are many places where you can find inspiration (youtube.com for example), but the best person who inspires is the Holy Spirit. He is your helper, so ask Him for the inspiration. Also ask for feedback from others in the dance group to ensure that the message is as clear as possible.

When you are creating a dance for people from other cultures and settings, there are a lot of things that you need to think about. If you want to win a person's trust you may need to adjust some things. Is the song supposed to speak to a 14-

year-old American girl or a 50-year-old Muslim woman from Ethiopia?

The cultural differences can be pretty large. Moves that are perceived as innocent in America can be offensive in another culture. Also certain types of music that work well in the western world might not be appreciated at all in Asia. In some cultures a harder type of music is completely unthinkable. It is important to think about this if you really want to succeed in reaching people. Nothing should take the focus away from the message.

- If you are to dance for people that you know come from another culture, think about the moves so that they are not offensive or provocative.

- Set the degree of difficulty for the dance according to the dancers' skill. It is better to use simpler moves that you can perform tightly than to use difficult moves that you cannot really master.

- Work with your body language and mimic. This is important in order to make the message reach the people. Your facial expressions will reinforce what you want to say.

When you have come this far the only thing you need to do is to begin practicing. Set a goal, a date when you need to be finished with the dance and then begin to practice. If there are some in the dance group that have never danced before, it is important that you take your time. Everyone can learn how to dance; it just takes a little longer for those who are not used to it. It is better to have many short practice times more often, than to practice four hours once a month. The moves need to sink in. The concept of "sleeping on it" is actually a tactic that works well in regards to dance. It is also important to encourage and spur one another on, in order to give that little extra, ensuring that the dance becomes as good and tight as possible.

Finally, do not forget the most important thing. If you are a dance team that is sincere about conveying your message with all of your heart, this will make a greater impression than if you are just technically capable. People see through you, they see what attitude you have. If you have prayed for the people that you are going to dance for and really long to present Jesus for them, that will shine through! In 2 Corinthians 5:14 it says that Christ's love compels us. If He is the driving force behind what you do, you will succeed.

### Some Practical Tips for a Performance

- Think about your clothes. Never have a deep neckline nor show your belly when you are dancing on stage. A good way to test the stage clothes is to lift your arms as high as possible and then squat. Repeat the procedure a couple of times. If neither belly or back is showing after 5-6 times, the clothes will work on stage. You should never have to adjust the shirt or your hairdo during a dance; the clothes must be able to handle all the moves.

- Never mind if the dance is not 100% perfect half an hour before you are to go up on stage. It is better to pray during this time than to practice until the last minute. It is more important that you have the right focus on stage than that you dance a perfect dance.

- If you should forget the moves, just continue to dance. If you make a mistake but look secure, the audience will think that is how it is supposed to be. It is only when you stop and look insecure that people will notice.

- Stay focused from the time you enter the stage until you get off, even if you are not dancing the whole time. If you stand on the side and watch your friend dancing the solo, you are still a part of the per formance. Do not relax and scratch yourself on the leg, the audience can still see you. When you are 100% focused, God can use you 100%.

**Remember!**

- Think through the purpose of the dance.
- Choose a song that suits the occasion.
- Think about the moves.
- Adjust the level of difficulty.
- Have the right focus.

Believe that what you do is of importance, even if you are not a professional. God sees our heart. If you have the attitude that you are going to reach people with the message, you will succeed. Think big, do not limit God! He has great dreams and plans and He is really creative! Make sure that you think about yourself the same way that God thinks about you.

## The Purpose for Dance

In the spring of 2006 Mission SOS traveled to Harar in Ethiopia with a large team from SOS Mission Bible College. Harar is seen by many as the fourth most holy city of Islam and the majority who live there are Muslims. Before we traveled we practiced a dance to an Ethiopian worship song. The festival musicians also practiced the song so that they would be able to sing it in the local language.

During that trip we experienced how effective dance really is. Many of the inhabitants were skeptical to the very fact that we had traveled there and they really did not want to listen to us. But when we danced in the city and on the festival stage in their manner, to their own music and with their kind of moves, they relaxed! The wall that was between us Christians and the non-Christians came crashing down to the beat of the music, and we were able to dance, sing and laugh together.

Later in the festival we saw the whole audience, a crowd of thousands of people, dance with us in our dance and we realized that the prejudice was gone! The dance had created a path into the hearts of the people of Harar. The tension between Muslims and Christians disappeared and we were able to rejoice and have a successful festival. This is what God created dance for!

# DRAMA

By Maria Evermin

In the Gospels we repeatedly see Jesus using pictures and parables to clarify the Word for the people so that they could understand and receive it. Just look at the 15th chapter of the Gospel of Luke, in which He talked about the sheep that was found, the lost coin and the prodigal son. These are amazing parables and pictures that clearly explain God's heart for the lost and his joy when a person returns to Him and receives salvation. Jesus constantly painted messages in pictures for people through the words that He spoke. The people who listened could envision the story in front of them.

This is what we do when we use drama. We paint the Gospel for people, we create a picture for them to see, understand and receive the love God has revealed to them, so that they may be able to receive Jesus as their Savior.

I love to preach and present Jesus in a relevant and distinct way through drama. It is an incredible tool and it constantly challenges me to think in new terms to be able to reach yet another person with the good news.

Drama, or street theater, as we also call it (I will continue to use the word drama in this text) in Mission SOS, is a pure sermon in itself. It is also a tool to help the preacher prepare the ground for the word that will be sent out, opening up people's hearts and pulling down the glory of God. When language becomes a barrier and people have a hard time understanding what we preach, then it is so wonderful to be able to use this tool.

It is the most awesome thing to be a part of a drama! You can see in the eyes of the people that they are listening to what is being presented. You can see them begin to understand as they watch a drama which paints Jesus and the cross, and then watch the tears run down their cheeks as they feel the presence of God and run to the front of the stage to receive salvation! When I then think that one day we will stand before the throne and praise Jesus with that person who was saved after the drama we performed that day, my eyes are filled with tears too. What grace it is to be able to do what I do! For it is only grace and nothing else that enables us to be God's tools in these End Times.

## My Story

To use drama for evangelism is really an exciting challenge for me. It all began about six years ago. Johannes Amritzer asked me if I would think about becoming the Drama Director for Mission SOS. I had, up to that point, worked with media and production for a couple of years within Mission SOS; and for me, it was a very big step to start up and lead everything that had to do with drama. Another thing was that never during my upbringing had I had anything to do with theater or even seen a production, whether live or on TV. I didn't know what the concept of theater meant, much less what you could do with it, especially with the purpose of evangelism.

During my first years in Mission SOS, we had done two dramas at different festivals. I had participated a little in one of the dramas, but that is all the experience I had. These two dramas were the only ones I somewhat knew; they made up the foundation for everything I knew about drama. When Johannes Amritzer asked me, I told him I would think about it.

I went home and prayed about it and asked God what He thought about it, and I received a very clear yes from Him – so clear that I could not hesitate. So I went back to Johannes a couple of days later and told him I would do it! The ground beneath my feet swayed! I went back home, threw myself on God and cried! I did not understand why He would want me to begin working with drama. I who knew nothing about this, I had never had anything to do with this or done anything creative, I did not even have the passion for drama. I just could not get it together. But I said, "Okay, God, I have been obedient to You. You said go, and so I did, but now I ask that You reveal this subject to me, that You give me visions, dreams, pictures, and all the guidance I need to lead and develop the drama ministry in Mission SOS. I want Your passion for this, help me to view drama the way You view it: as an important tool to preach the Gospel with and to reach the unreached peoples." When I was finished praying, I felt that this, if anything, was walking on water!

Only a couple of days after I had agreed, I received invitations to two different churches in Sweden to come and teach drama. I accepted and since then, the invitations have just continued to come. I now also produce new dramas, both for Sweden and for festivals among unreached peoples, and I lead a drama course at our Bible College.

It is a lot of work, but I love it! What makes walking on water so wonderful is that you become completely dependent upon God. He has given me so many pictures, dreams and ideas on how to do things. He tells me what I should think about when I teach, how I can solve problems that arise, what methods I should use. I still smile to myself and wonder, "How did all of this actually take place?"

I remember the first drama course I held. I did not know what I was supposed to say or do, but when I opened my mouth, the words just came. I was able to instruct the students on how they were supposed to act and think. After finishing the first lesson, a girl came up to me, and told me that she had been studying theater for a couple of years. She told me that the methods and the way of thinking I had taught was some kind of well known Russian method and that she admired me for all my knowledge in the subject! I was surprised and very encouraged by what she told me and I thought to myself, "Thank you, God, for Your knowledge and wisdom!" Imagine how everything is possible for the one who believes! If I can, you can!

If God has called you to something, then He will give you the power and the knowledge to be able to do it. You simply have to begin to do it and believe God for the rest. He will help you do so much more, as long as you have a pure, willing and humble heart.

It is important to remember, though, that being alone is not being strong. Do not be prideful, but be very humble and thankful for the thing that God has accomplished through you and for what He wants to bring you into. Build a team around you and invest in them. Find people that you can develop into becoming more skillful than yourself and who will be able to go further than yourself within drama. The advantage of being a team is that you are more effective, and you can often help each other in developing dramas in a much better way than had you done it by yourself. The first years that I worked with drama I did it by myself, but lately I have been so privileged to have a couple of people work with me closely. A good thing about working together in a team is that it is not one person who gets the admiration for the work that has been done; rather there are many helping out. This helps to keep us humble and thankful before God.

## A Biblical Foundation

I have already mentioned that Jesus constantly used parables when He preached to the masses and to His disciples. A couple of years ago, God showed me that the work I do resembles a lot of what Moses did in his time. Just to pick an example, we can read the story about Moses in Exodus 25:9; 39:32-43; and 40:16, 33-35.

Moses received visions, pictures and clear instructions on how he was to go about building the tabernacle. He followed the heavenly blue print he had on the inside down to the smallest detail, without diverting from it at any point. Moses built with excellence and had an enormous stringency for the details. When they later dedicated the temple, God's glory descended on the tabernacle and filled it. God was there! Isn't this an awesome picture of how God works!?

Our assignment is to follow what God has given us, put it into practice and always handle it with excellence. We are simply to use the gift or gifts we have received. Begin with what you have, what God has spoken to you about or the little you know, and God will do the rest.

## Creating

Giving birth to a drama and then producing it is something very exciting. I begin by focusing on the ones the drama is directed towards. Is it a specific group of people in your society, is it unreached peoples or maybe an entire nation? That is why research needs to be done on what their culture is like, their clothes and the different kinds of problems that they have in their society. After that I usually pray and fast and then I ask God about the spiritual situation over the group of people I want to preach to. Maybe they live under some kind of oppression, such as depression, hopelessness or drugs. Then God wants us to break that influence and proclaim freedom instead! This process must take the time that is needed. I ask God for ideas, pictures, dreams and also creativity to accomplish all of this. He knows the heart of every person and knows everything; therefore it is extremely important to follow what He says.

Sometimes I get a picture; other times I see the whole finished drama on the inside of me. Next time I just get an idea or a part of the drama. But often it does not take a long time before it is all clear to me, such as the story in the drama and how I am supposed to do it.

Then the work begins. Just like Moses, I need to realize the picture I have received. Practical problems, such as sound, lighting, props and everything within the production have to be solved and the choreography needs to be complete for the drama to be considered whole. I begin to look for people who can play the different roles and then begin to work with them.

Seeing the picture which I have seen on the inside become a reality is very stimulating. When the drama is later being performed before an audience and I notice that people understand what is being preached and want to receive Jesus; when God's presence and power is there, I know that I have accomplished my task.

## Thinking in New Terms

Try to think about blowing your limitations and be outside of the box while you are creating new productions. Do not always do as you usually do. Change the way you are thinking, creating and what you are acting upon. Dare to think of something new within every area. Be creative! Dare to use things from many different areas in life. I, for example, love to use multi-media in every form, or dance and live music together with drama. This gives such variety to the drama and can speak to many different people or just help make the message more distinct.

One thing that I usually think about to make myself realize that I do not have any limitations is, "I can do everything and I can use everything." Then I pray for God's help to realize it all. Think about what you can do and use, not about what you cannot. Then God will give you the solution for your problems. Simply put, become a problem solver! Throw yourself on God if things do not work out, be dependent on Him! It is an adventure to be led by Him and you never know what is going to happen; but one thing I do know: it will be very good!

## Acting

Something that is very important when you create dramas is to make everything very clear, simple and sharp. This applies to the script but also to what everyone in the team is saying through their body language and mimic when they act. Just as a musician needs to practice his instrument, we need to practice our body language and our mimic.

In every part of the drama you need to think about what you actually want to say. Ask yourself, "What is the message?" From there you go through different feelings, body languages and mimics that you want to use to paint that message as clearly as possible for the audience. That is why picture language and the details, which make up the entirety of the drama, are so important.

What you do needs to be planned out from the beginning and thoroughly carried out to the end. Just remember that if something in the script is unclear or if someone in the team has a fuzzy mimic, the whole drama will become unclear, which in turn will make the people who listen confused over what you're trying to say.

Regardless of what level of skill your drama achieves, the

message that it preaches has to be clear. None of us wants to preach an unclear Gospel or have it on our consciences that we have "burned" an audience, so that they never want to watch another drama or listen to another sermon. We have a responsibility when we act, to do what we do with great sincerity! It is not about me but about the salvation of other people! I usually say that when you act, act as if it was your first and only time. It is dangerous to fall into habits and merely begin performing everything out of plain routine. I usually think before a performance that I may never again get the chance to preach to these people again.

We do not know what will happen to the person in the audience after the outreach or the festival meeting that we have held. He/she might, in the worst case scenario, be hit by a car just seconds after and die. If so, that would mean that I have had the chance to preach and reveal the Gospel to that person, but did not take hold of that opportunity! Our focus needs to be to preach for one person all the time, not for the masses. I usually recommend to everyone I train that they pick out a person in the audience to preach for when they then perfrom the drama. In that way what we do will not become a routine, instead it becomes more personal.

In Matthew 10:8 it says that we are to freely give what we've received as a gift, and in 2 Timothy 4:2, Paul says to preach in season and out of season. This is something we all must take hold of when we act and even when we live our daily lives. We do not know when we have the greatest impact!

## Ability to Identify With

Another thing that I focus a lot on and that I really think is important to work on, is first feeling the emotions that you want to convey, and then making the audience feel what you feel. Simply live out the role that you are playing. The fact that you dare to show anger, evil and hate if you are acting the devil, makes people feel the very thing you are acting out. It is important that you dare to show feelings and give it everything you have got. When it is about other people's salvation, you need to put yourself aside and give of yourself, it is worth the risk of exposing yourself.

Even if you have to ignore your pride and prestige from time to time, that is a good thing. If you have the focus and the passion for people, you will want to do whatever it takes for at least one more person to be saved, as Paul so well expressed it in 1 Corinthians 9:19-22. Then you are able to give of yourself a lot easier.

A lot in our world is superficial today. Everything is about looks, money and career; that is why I think it is even more important to show your feelings when you act and also to mean what you "say." Hypocrisy is one of the worst things there is. When you are sending out a message through a drama but do not mean it or are not living purely, then the whole drama will fall, and the glory and power of God will not be there.

> *For the kingdom of God is not a matter of talk but of power.*
>
> **1 Corinthians 4:20**

God is the only one who can save a person but we can be channels for His power. What we need to do is work on our salvation daily and examine ourselves, especially our hearts. When you stand on stage, it is good to remember that we represent everything that God is. People will not only see what we do, but also what we have in our hearts. In other words, you preach with everything that is within you.

## Illustrating

We also work with illustrating sermons. This means that we dramatize what is being said with short improvised illustrations. Often there is not a lot of time to prepare for this, so what I do is develop an idea from the sermon that will be preached and then communicate that idea on stage. Sometimes I need several people to participate, in addition to myself, and maybe a few props as well. It is very challenging and a true adventure to improvise while someone is preaching.

This is also something you can practice at home. For example, you can have a friend speak while you act out what they are saying. Do not forget that what you do needs to be as clear and sharp as in a drama. It is harder to illustrate a sermon than to act in a drama, because in a drama you have had the time to practice your body language, mimic, and feeling. But when you improvise, you never know what is coming up next – that is why you need to be good at all this beforehand. It is just as important to be distinct in your performance when you improvise something, as when you are acting in a drama that you have rehearsed over and again.

## Becoming Skillful

In order to become a better actor, there are some practical things you can do. You can study the people around you and study different movie or theater actors. You can search on the Internet or read books in which people describe and give different exercises on body language, mimic, how to master your body and balance. When you discover someone who is very distinct in expressing certain body movements or feelings, then memorize that. Practice achieving the same feeling through your body language.

Act in front of your friends who maybe are not that creative and see what they think about your body language. If what you want to convey is very clear, that is awesome; but if they stand like huge question marks, wondering what you are doing and what you are trying to say, you might have to practice a bit more.

Always strive to become better! We must remember though, that maybe not everyone is a star at acting. Some of us need to practice more and others less, but we can all preach! Give drama a chance. Maybe you have more talent than you thought – but you will not know until you have given it an honest chance.

## Final Words

Below are some points that are good to think about when you work with drama:

- From the moment the music begins until the very end, you have to act. Begin acting before the drama even begins and stop acting after everything is over. Otherwise you will give the impression of not meaning what you do. It will instead seem like you are only carrying a mask and not really caring about what you do. Remember that there are always several people in the audience that are watching you in particular. Whether you act a lot or a little during the drama, you still need to do your best the whole way through.

- Do not drift off in your thoughts and begin to think about other things while you are acting; the people in the audience will notice this right away. Stay focused all the time. In Mission SOS we have this expression: "Concentration is anointing." It is good to remind yourself of that.

- No one knows that you have made a mistake until you show it with your face and body language. Whatever happens, even if props break or the music skips, keep going! The expression "the show must go on" is also good to remember.

- Do not forget to encourage each other in the team. When you need to criticize, give constructive criticism.

- Pray a lot! Do not rely on your experience or your ability. Allow the Holy Spirit to be your teacher. Once again, stay away from routine!

- Look at the people when you are acting, do not look over their heads. Communicate with them. It will help both you and them feel the emotion and understand the message.

- When you want to use scenery and other props, do not use too much or too little. Keep in mind that you should use only what is needed to create the feeling you want. You need to do this especially if you are doing an outreach. Because then you are not able to take a whole truckload of costumes with you.

Good luck preaching Jesus with everything that is in you!

## JOINT CLOSURE

We now want to challenge you who are longing to preach and convey the message in a creative way. Start up a dance, song or a theater group! Are you a bunch of people in your church that are longing to testify and preach to the people in your city? Get started! It is okay if there are only a few of you in the beginning, the important thing is that you get started! It is when you walk in faith that God will help you. Maybe your church is doing a community outreach six months from now where you will have one or more creative elements. You do not have to do things every week, begin where you are.

## Practical Ideas on How to Get Started

- Gather everyone you think might be interested in being a part of your group.
- Pray that God will give you inspiration and ideas
- Sit down together and brainstorm, dare to think new!
- Seek help from God, so that you can present the message in the best way possible.
- Set goals for what you are going to produce and book a date for when you will perform.
- Prepare well by practicing a lot.
- When it is time, invite a lot of people, especially your non-Christian friends.

The Holy Spirit will give you ideas and dreams of how to preach to the people around you in different creative ways. Maybe you can perform a multi-number that is about salvation, which is perfect to show at a school at Easter time. Or perform a dance that draws a lot of young people at the youth center a Friday night, and then one of you can get up and give your testimony.

Give what you have received and do not compare yourself with others. Never think that you are not good enough, that you are not talented enough or that you do not have good enough ideas. The Holy Spirit is creativity personified. He can give you that song that reaches your city and the hearts of your friends.

> *For the eyes of the LORD range throughout the earth to strengthen those whose hearts are fully committed to him.*
>
> **2 Chronicles 16:9a**

It does not say that He is going to help those with talent; it says that He will help those who have a committed heart. It is not about who you are, or what you are able to do – it is about the attitude of your heart and what He is able to do. With God everything is possible!

## A Glimpse from Our Daily Lives

I take another gulp from my water bottle and wipe the sweat from my forehead. I can feel the hot rays from the sun searching for my already sun-burned skin while I am standing in the shade of a tree. It is afternoon on the third day of our festival, and in just a couple of minutes the festival meeting will kick off. The local singers and musicians from the area are wrapping up their performances and around me curious and expectant people are dancing to the finishing tones. They look at me with interested gazes and I try to greet them and talk to them. I speak a few words that I have learned in their language. I watch several people arrive, a couple of young people run past me in order to come as close as possible to the stage. The dust whirls in their trail and I look to see what is happening below the platform. Our singers and musicians are warming up and the drama team is changing into their costumes and helping each other with the make-up.

All of a sudden everything takes off! The music begins to flow from the speakers that we have rented and I can literally feel the vibrations from the base tones that are being played.

I watch how the people beside me sing along in the festival songs that by now are well known to them. When the dancers step up and do moves to the different choruses, the whole sea of people roars and begins to dance to the music. At this point I am rejoicing over the feeling that we are one people – not two – having a festival, regardless of our skin color and cultural differences. Soaked with sweat, I also dance and laugh together with my newly found friends.

Songs, different dances and multi-numbers quickly follow one after the other without breaks in between. I see the dancers, the drama people and musicians taking turns changing behind and under the stage. The tempo is high. There are many drama clothes that need changing into and a lot of make-up that needs to be put on; everything has to work.

The team quickly checks the program, a piece of paper nailed to the side of the stage, for any last minute changes. During the festival, anything can happen. There could be a downpour, a storm or something else that could disturb the program. The creative people have to be constantly alert for the evangelist. If he wants to step up and preach earlier than planned, we cannot lose the people who have come. A festival is also a war for the salvation of the souls of people.

The drama team once again bow their heads and pray where they stand waiting to enter the stage. Without a warning the drama begins and at once people press closer to the stage to be able to see everything that is going on.

The singers, musicians and dancers are fully focused on what is happening and I can see how they are praying in tongues for the people and for the drama that is being performed. I feel tears burning when Jesus and the cross are explained. At the end of the drama, when Jesus is resurrected from the dead, I am no longer the only one with tears streaming down my cheeks.

Immediately after the drama, the evangelist steps up to the platform and begins to preach the Gospel. He illustrates many of his stories with the help of different creative team members. After a while the sea of people do not want to wait any longer, they have comprehended the love of God and they want Jesus!

A salvation invitation is given and all around me people run to the altar to give their lives to the only true God! The singers and musicians return to the platform and begin to sing wonderful Jesus songs, releasing a mighty presence of God. After the evangelist has led the people in a prayer of healing and deliverance, miracles begin to take place and evil spirits leave people.

I quickly move over to the altar and begin to anoint people with oil and pray short, faith-filled prayers. The deaf begin to hear; the lame walk and the blind receive their sight. After a while I hear an invitation go out for baptism in the Holy Spirit and the people turn their faces towards heaven and almost immediately some people standing next to me begin to pray in new tongues. I watch how they lift their hands in beautiful worship to God. After about two hours of wonderful, intense prayer, healing prayers and deliverance ministry, the people begin to make their way back home and the festival ground grows quiet.

I pause for a second and look down at my hands, smeared with oil. I turn my gaze toward the pitch black sky and express, from the depths of my heart, "Thank you, thank you, Jesus!" Imagine that I am a part of doing the Great Commission, that I am playing a part in all this!

CHAPTER 8

By Peter Almqvist

# Signs & Wonders Festivals

## The Combine Harvester for the Large Fields

*Meanwhile, when a crowd of many thousands had gathered, so that they were trampling on one another, Jesus began to speak…*

**Luke 12:1a**

One by one, they had gathered on the large open field at the outskirts of the city. A rumble of excited voices is heard. Everyone is so expectant over what is about to take place this evening. One person has come to the meeting out of simple curiosity, having seen all the posters around the city. Another has arrived, dragged by a neighbor who, the night before, experienced a healing power that set him free from years of pain. A third person has come with a longing to find the meaning of life, to be delivered from darkness and depression. Yet another has come in pure apathy and, on his way to the field, cried at the top of his voice towards heaven: "God, if you exist, show yourself to me!" The list goes on. All of them have come for different reasons, but they have a joint goal for the evening. They want to see if God exists and if He is able to meet them in their situation and if He cares for them specifically.

Where have you ended up? Well, in the middle of a festival among an unreached people group, probably somewhere in what is called the 10/40 window. That is the area that lies between the 10th and the 40th latitude north of the Equator, between Morocco in the West and Indonesia in the East. It is within this area that most of the people groups who have still not heard the best news in the world live. This is the area of the world that Mission SOS focuses on. We breathe these unreached peoples and live to see them changed by Jesus Himself. In order to have a better insight for what is happening in front of your eyes, let us go back about nine months in time and take a look to see how it all begins.

A Signs and Wonders Festival always begins on our knees before our God. When we are starting to plan a festival, we seek God and ask Him to lead us to areas with unreached peoples. It is not as simple as just buying an airplane ticket and flying to a new country.

The very first thing that needs to happen after the Holy Spirit has given us a green light into a certain region, is that we seek someone who will partner with us in the place where we are going. These partners are the ones who will stay there after we have returned home, and it is they who will be responsible for the large and important task of training disciples. Praying with people to salvation is only the beginning of the task; discipleship is the next. We leave this incredible, important part of the job to the local churches that are in the nearby area. I need to stress the point that Mission SOS does not go to an area if we are not first prepared to plant one or several new churches. This usually is a natural continuation of the festival.

## The Early Preparations

Let us return to our trip. After we have received a green light from the Holy Spirit, we send out a team to scout out the area to find the best place for a large campaign. During the same trip we connect with the local pastors and spiritual leaders to first and foremost share the vision that God has given us for the region and the peoples who live there.

After presenting the vision we always try to immediately put together an organizing committee with the assignment of working with the daily planning before the festival. A person is appointed as the national festival coordinator. He becomes the motor and the one who is in contact with all the different departments that are needed for a successful festival.

Implementing a festival is far from being a one man's job. What is needed is a diligent team of co-workers who all do whatever it takes and sometimes even more than that to get the job done. During the years, we have put together a festival team which has become very tight; each person knows his or her role. A close, experienced team is a great help in the daily work.

At the same time, however, it can also become a great danger. We need to constantly pray for God's hand to rest on the work. We must all learn to trust the anointing that God gives more than we trust the experience we gain through the years. The anointing breaks the yoke, while the experience will either help or hinder us. We have put together a festival manual that is meticulously followed during the planning stages. If needed, it is translated to a local language, in order to make it easier for everyone involved. Within the committee, every person is given a responsibility for a certain department; today we have 13 departments beyond that of the local festival coordinator. They are as follows:

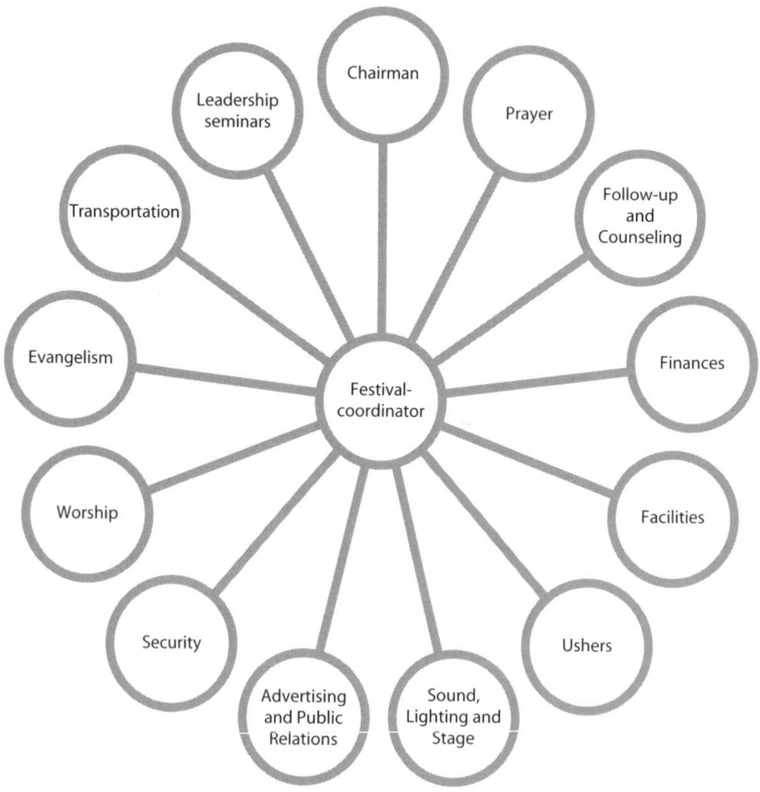

During the months that lead up to the festival, these departments will have unequal workloads with differing intensity. Let uss take the PR department as an example: their most intense time period will be starting one month before the festival, and then they will increase until the festival begins. For the people working with the engineering, it's quite the opposite. In the beginning their job is mainly to gather different offers, but it reaches its peak when it is time to rig everything up at the festival ground, run the event and then tear it down after the festival is completed.

The most important thing in the early stages is to create an awareness of the festival. We always begin by mobilizing all the churches in the region – and we cooperate with everyone who believes in and preaches the full Gospel. We do not work only within a certain denomination; rather we work on a very broad scale. Our national festival coordinator gathers the working committee and together a mobilization campaign is planned in the city or in the region. It starts with the Christians. In an early stage all the pastors are invited to a vision-casting meeting in order to make them feel a part of what is happening. Through this assimilation process, they are then better enabled to carry the festival themselves.

## Creating Awareness or Marketing

After having mobilized the Christians, the phase begins that is directed towards the public; this is called public relations or PR. Here there are many roads to choose from. It all depends on what works best in the chosen region. TV, for example, is huge in larger cities, while radio is better in rural areas as well as in poorer areas. To create awareness among the public, people need to be more or less bombarded by advertisement about the festival. We print up colorful posters, hand out flyers, put up banners and make use of large billboards. We try to do everything we can so that no one can miss out on the festival and that Jesus is on the way to their city or region. Sometimes we have advertised the festival with the text: "Free healing for both Christians and Muslims." That is when we have seen the most results. People come to the festival site hungry for their miracle.

Parallel with this initial phase, our international board is working with fund raising to finance the festival. The board constantly works on finding partners who want to stand alongside us in the large global harvest of the end times. We are so thankful to all the people and churches, companies and organizations who have stood with us through the years and who are directly involved in all the victories we have seen for the kingdom of God around the world.

On the home front, teams that will go out and evangelize the streets during the festival week are trained. Our dance, drama and music instructors make sure that we have a well trained team with us that will reach the heart of the people. If you can reach the heart of the people, then you have succeeded. I would like to stress that we never travel to a place to preach against something or someone, but that everything we talk about, and in different ways visualize in a creative ways, is Jesus. We want to lift Jesus high among all people – then He will draw the people to Himself.

Let us get back to the work of the organizing committee and the preparations on site. At an early stage the festival site is secured by signing a contract between the parties concerned. Here we have two choices. The first alternative is the use of a stadium. There are many positive benefits with this; there is always enough electricity for all the engineering and besides that, there are always enough toilets. The main disadvantage that I view is that stadiums are built to keep people inside. By this I mean that it is difficult to maneuver the people, to move them from one place to another, for example during a salvation invitation. At the same time it is easy to have everything under control in regards to security, but you will have real challenges when the people want to respond to the Gospel.

If the festival is to be held in a rural area, it is rare to find a stadium. Then we will have to choose the second alternative, which is actually the better of the two: an open field. The people can easily get there and back; they can even stay at an anonymous safe distance if they want to. In addition to this, the people can also respond so much easier and make their way to the platform to pray a salvation prayer with hundreds of others.

When the local pastors have caught the vision and become carriers of it and the festival site is secured, our media department in Stockholm takes over and begins to produce advertising material. Layouts for posters and flyers are made, and, if needed, TV jingles as well. This material is then sent to the local coordinator who makes sure that it is printed.

About four weeks before the festival, the job begins of wallpapering the city or area with posters. When this is done, it should be impossible to be unaware that there will be a festival in the area. There are various ways that this can be accomplished. Usually, there are teams that go out every night putting up new posters. Sometimes we use the help of a helicopter to drop tens of thousands of flyers over the city. While the festival is being advertised all over the city, the local Christians are being trained for different tasks. As I've mentioned before, this is far from being a one man's job or a one man's show.

When the people arrive by the thousands at the festival site, we want them to feel safe and secure. All our trained ushers will make sure that the people find their places and then all the security guards will ensure that we do not have any incidents. In the history of Mission SOS we have not had many serious incidents or accidents in connection with the festivals. The most serious thing that has happened was outside a stadium in Southern Bulgaria, when 50 people had to be taken to the hospital. The Gospel is confrontational and when this Kingdom of light encounters the darkness of this world, it causes a reaction in one way or another.

## Spiritual Warfare

During all festivals, at different places and among different people groups, we have really seen how God confirms His word. Mark chapter 16 comes alive every time the Gospel is preached. People come for completely different reasons but with one thing in common: to seek the One who can put everything back into place - the Creator Himself.

Prayer lays the foundation for everything God wants to do. It is not only in the beginning phase that we throw ourselves on our knees before the throne of God. During the time of preparations we need the hand of God and His favor on all the details. The local churches arrange prayer nights and gather the Christians to councils of war. It is here that the victory is won. When we unite and corporately cry out to God for a breakthrough and for the salvation of people, we see how an entire region is completely changed by the power of God. There is nothing comparable to when the Gospel enters a region and lifts, not only individuals, but entire communities from the mire.

In many of these untouched places there is a clear and distinct spiritual openness. This is often recognized through strong manifestations in the people who live under the influence of evil spirits. During our festivals we take care of all those who are manifesting and pray them through to freedom. Then we pray with them to salvation and baptism in the Holy Spirit before they leave to go back home. We have so many stories about people who have been set free after years of demonic bondage.

Behind the stage we always have a tent that we call "The Demon Clinic." Everyone who is manifesting is brought here for deliverance. Here we have a special team that is ready to receive and help these wonderful people and cast out the evil spirits. The deliverance warriors have a special place in Mission SOS. Without them the devil would have been able to many times steal the focus from the Gospel, a focus needed for people to come out of darkness into light.

If we are in a region with long distances to the surrounding villages, we always rent vehicles that can transport people to the festival site. This is a huge project. We make sure that vehicles, usually buses, go to the different existing villages and meet up people that cannot get there by themselves or who cannot afford to travel on their own. Many times we watch how people receive all they can get from God during the festival meeting before they get back on the bus to travel home again. For many of them this is a life changing moment. They will not settle for less than God meeting them where they are.

## And So the Time Has Come…

As time passes by and the festival is approaching, a rising expectation becomes more noticeable among the participating churches. In one place local worship teams are practicing, in another prayer warriors are praying. In yet another place ushers and security staff are being trained. Everyone is being inspired and challenged to invite a non-Christian to the festival. It could be a colleague from work, a friend, relative or neighbor. Everyone attempts to bring someone with them.

So finally the great day arrives – the evening when the festival starts. Now we are standing there in the midst of the sea of people, in the dust, looking over the stage. We are met by the deafening sound bursting from the speakers and we stand beside people who carry an expectation for what is going to take place; once again it is an enormous feeling that is hard to describe in words. To stand there in an open field that has the capacity to hold tens of thousands of people is something extraordinary.

On stage is a local music team that leads the masses of people in traditional songs. Usually, they start up to one hour before scheduled time to draw people to the site. Sound attracts people and people attract more people. The crowd increases in size during the evening and grows from evening to evening, until it peaks at the concluding meeting. By then the rumor about all that Jesus is doing has reached the whole city or area.

People are coming by the droves to the festival. Succeeding the local worship team, a well produced program is taking shape on stage. Musicians, actors and dancers, one after the other, enter the stage – they all try to create a festive atmosphere. The songs are many times sung in one of the local languages; they are happy songs with a high tempo. The singers attempt to reach the hearts of the audience. All of a sudden the music is cut off and a professional dance is performed on stage. Before the crowd can stop applauding, the quietness after the dance is shattered by a roar – it is time for a drama about the crucifixion.

The actors stage the bloodiest act of love the world knows. Jesus is whipped, beaten and hung on a cross. Shortly after that He resurrects and gives salvation and healing to the people. By now the audience stands quietly with their eyes sharply fixed on the platform. The preacher, in this case Johannes Amritzer, takes hold of the microphone and shouts with a hoarse voice, "Hallelujah!" The people respond immediately. Now we are having a festival for real!

## After the Message

The crowd listens attentively to the message about a God who cares and who came down to us human beings to take our mistakes on Himself and to die in our place. When the question is asked if there is anyone who would like to receive Him, hands are raised all over the field. The ushers let down the rope that has been placed around an area in front of the platform. They are ready to receive the crowd of people who will soon run to the front. Evangelist Johannes Amritzer then leads them in a prayer of salvation before they are led to an area behind the stage that has been prepared for the follow-up work. There is already an army of trained follow-up workers in place, who are ready to write down the contact information of every person who gives their life to Jesus. After this, everyone receives the book Saved in the Last Days as a gift. It has already been translated into the local language and printed in a large edition. This short booklet explains for the newly saved what has happened as they received salvation and continues with the first steps in the Christian faith.

After a completed festival all of the follow-up cards are divided between the different participating churches and that is really when the job itself begins. Praying with people to salvation is the easy part. If there are not enough churches or if they do not have the capacity to take care of the harvest, we as an organization step in and plant at least one completely new church. Every festival is unique in its own way, but we always see how churches grow afterwards and most of the time new churches are planted as well – either as independent churches, or as daughter churches to already existing churches.

While the newly saved are taken care of, the musicians return to the stage and play. When most names have been written down and booklets have been handed out, it is time to pray for the sick. Many have come for a miracle. But remember, my friend that the greatest miracle of all is to be saved, to become free and forgiven and enter the original plan that God has for your life.

## Jesus Heals the Sick

All the sick are then invited to the area in front of the stage. The team that has traveled to the festival is now standing in a line front of the stage, facing the people and they are ready to minister to the people. Everyone who comes to the front receives prayer and now things begin to happen. God confirms His Word and people who have arrived with the expectation to receive healing, are immediately healed. There are many who are instantly healed from their ailment – it could be the man with severe back pain who has not been able to walk upright or lie down, or the woman who was born blind. For God there is no miracle that is harder than another. According to His Word everything was finished on the cross and He longs to release His healing power in these wonderful people.

Once again, to the left of the stage a special area is reserved. This time it is a station for healing documentation. We are so happy for everything Jesus does and we love to report every miracle that takes place. Everything is written down, people's photos are taken and they are videotaped. If there is a clear and powerful miracle that has taken place, we bring them up on stage and have them testify before the crowd. Let me point out that every miracle that takes place is equally wonderful; but an obvious miracle, such as a blind person who receives his sight, creates faith for others to believe that everything is possible.

The crowd is silenced when they see the man who works at the gas station standing on the platform. Everybody knows he cannot hear or speak. You can almost hear a pin drop. What is going to happen now? The man is asked about what has happened. He is making wild gestures to say that he is now able to hear sound in his ears. After testing him up on the stage and finding that he hears, the joy in the audience knows no limits. They wildly rejoice over what Jesus is doing. When the man is also able to form sound out of his previously quiet mouth we are met with a deafening roar. The crowd does not know where to go or what to do. The joy knows no limits; everyone is dancing, singing and rejoicing.

Our Jesus is so wonderful. He loves to show Himself to people who seek Him with a pure heart. He loves to help and lift people. In Mission SOS, we have the best job in the world.

Bringing the Gospel in this manner to people who have never heard cannot be described in words. As we approach our landing, we see how the people leave the festival site in large crowds after the final meeting, praising God with loud voices. This place will never be the same again. The Gospel is the power of God to salvation. It breaks through completely closed regions and it has enough power to break through any wall or levy. There are no impossible fields or hopeless cases, only a lack of love. In Mission SOS we have decided that we are going to love people to heaven. We love to see Jesus perform miracles and watch how He is able to completely change a person's life. What no man can do, Jesus accomplishes so easily.

Thank you for following along on this short journey; I hope that you have received a small insight into how a festival among an unreached people group is realized. Mass evangelism is a very impactful tool that God uses around the globe. Harvesters that are able to plow through the large fields are needed more than ever, but it is just as significant to go fishing with your fishing rod and catch an old pike. He might have been waiting for a long period of time. Maybe it is his time right now. God does not look first hand at quantity. He cares for the one person just as much as for the crowd at the stadium.

We so often think in human terms. God has an eagle's perspective and we have the perspective of a frog. But if we pray, God is able to lift us up to Himself and allow us to see things from His perspective. Then life becomes much more meaningful to live. Remember that God has called us to be fishers of men; it is not mentioned if the crowd is big or small. Let us love people to heaven – one by one!

# FINAL WORDS

No one knows who will listen when you raise your voice. Someone's daughter, a woman's husband, someone's best friend, a brother, a future prime minister… A you or a me.

Imagine yourself sitting in a park on a warm summer evening, with ice cream in your belly. You have just preached a succinct Gospel and now you are sitting in the grass with one or two or twenty and helping them pray a prayer of salvation… Someone dries a moist cheek; another is obviously focused because he does not want to stumble over the words at a moment like this. You let one eye peer over at the people – your new disciples. Someone allows his eye to peer over at you – his first real priest… Can you envision this?

No one can win everyone, but everyone can win one – what are you waiting for?

## About the Author

Johannes Amritzer is a powerful evangelist and Bible teacher who has traveled around the world for 17 years. He preaches the Gospel, mostly among people groups who have never before heard of Jesus Christ. Johannes and his wife Maria started Evangelical Mission SOS International in 1996. During their ministry they have seen tens of thousands of people receive Jesus as their Savior, healed in their bodies, baptized in the Holy Spirit and delivered from evil spirits. Mission SOS has its headquarters at SOS Church in Stockholm, Sweden where Johannes is the Lead Pastor.

## Other Books and Booklets by the Author:

- Musician Warrior King
- How Jesus Healed the Sick – and How You Can Too!
- Baptized in the Holy Spirit and Fire
- Practical Discipleship Training School
- Saved in the Last Days

For more information about Mission SOS or to order materials contact us at:

**Website** www.missionsos.com
**E-mail** usoffice@missionsos.org
**Phone** +1 412 487 7220